MARRIAGE 101

for

MEN

MARRIAGE 101

for

MEN

why
TAKING OUT THE TRASH
IS A TURN-ON

SHERRI MILLS

PLAIN SIGHT PUBLISHING
AN IMPRINT OF CEDAR FORT, INC.
SPRINGVILLE, UTAH

ISBN 13: 978-1-4621-1209-8

Published by Plain Sight Publishing, an imprint of Cedar Fort, Inc.
2373 W. 700 S., Springville, UT 84663
Distributed by Cedar Fort, Inc., www.cedarfort.com

LIBRARY OF CONGRESS CATALOGING-IN-PUBLICATION DATA

Mills, Sherri (Sherri M.), 1941- author.
 Marriage 101 : why taking out the trash is a turn-on / Sherri Mills.
   pages cm
 Includes bibliographical references.
 ISBN 978-1-4621-1209-8 (alk. paper)
 1. Marriage. I. Title.

 HQ734.M7134 2013
 306.81--dc23

                    2013003272

Cover design by Angela D. Olsen
Cover design © 2013 by Lyle Mortimer
Edited and typeset by Whitney A. Lindsley

Printed in the United States of America

10 9 8 7 6 5 4 3 2 1

I have no choice but to dedicate this book to my wonderful husband, Gerald. Throughout this whole process he has been behind me 100%. It hasn't been easy for him. He is retired now, and I work. When I come home, I go downstairs immediately and work on my marketing and my next book.

He did ask me with melancholy, "Are you going to keep writing?"

I told him that I had to write a book about divorce from a child's point of view. When I saw the look on his face, I knew that the book couldn't become all-consuming. I knew that he has to come first in my life, so I will ramble through the next book. If anyone deserves to come first, it is definitely him

SO THANK YOU, GERALD, WITH ALL MY LOVE.

Other books by Sherri Mills

I Almost Divorced My Husband, But I Went on Strike Instead

CONTENTS

CONTENTS

PRAISE FOR
MARRIAGE 101 FOR MEN

"This book is just what I have been looking for. It drives the point to young married couples who become disillusioned with their grandiose expectations of domestic life. Mills is brutally frank about the lifelong implications of divorce and its effect on children, something anyone considering divorce needs to realize. It is also an essential component to domestic violence counseling."

Dr. Greg Cowen, LCSW

"Author and hairdresser Sherri Mills has clocked more 'therapy' hours in her chair than I have in mine as a clinical psychologist. She has it all going on when it comes to making marriages survive and thrive! She's right on the money! Research shows that men who give a little more in the kitchen will likely get a little more in the bedroom. I celebrate Sherri's insight that it's not the division of labor that's most important but the unification of shared daily lives. Mutual marital investment offers the highest rate of return!"

Liz Hale, PhD

"Sherri explains this FAR better than I do, but doing housework is about fair distribution, and especially about ownership! You don't do dishes because it helps your wife—you do dishes because it's YOUR job. You need to take ownership of it and do it your way. Make your wife proud! But this isn't a one-way thing. Sherri also does a fabulous job teaching you how to help your wife understand that she doesn't need to control the parts of housework that are yours."

Chas Hathaway, author of *Marriage Is Ordained of God,*
but Who Came Up with Dating?

"Sherri Mills is at it again, balancing relationships and ultimately saving marriages. In *I Almost Divorced My Husband, But I Went On Strike Instead*, Mills opens up the conversation of balance in a marriage and in her follow up, *Marriage 101 for Men: Why Taking Out the Trash Is a Turn-On*, she tackles the intimacy puzzle head on. Easy to read, easy to understand, and even easy to implement, this is a must read for couples at all stages of their marriage. Thank you Sherri for taking a stand to save our marriages and families."

Stephanie Worlton, author of *Hope's Journey*

"Every household needs a copy of this book! Very well written. Author Sherri Mills points out many issues that have plagued marriages throughout the centuries. Her down-to-earth solutions are just what every husband needs to make their marriage painless and successful."

—Mandi Tucker Slack, author of *The Alias* and *Tide Ever Rising*

"This book proves an old (married) dog *can* learn new tricks."

Charlie Johnston:

"Sherri Mills, THANK YOU for your power-packed advice book. You treated with warmth and humor—and uncommon savvy—the hard lessons learned by common men (and women) that you listened to during your decades as a confidant, sounding board, and hairdresser."

—Louie, a skeptic turned fan

"Author Sherri Mills knows her topic and truly cares about her readers. Laugh with her. Rage with her. She shares a tested path to permanently more satisfying marriages. I am honored to edit her books."

—Elaine Rhode

"When a man shifts his perspective from 'helping' around the house to dividing ownership of household chores, he frees his wife to have the time, energy, and desire for a lot more togetherness, especially in the bedroom. I know . . .'"

—Jimmy Hicks, one whom Sherri has helped

"Sherri, thank you for putting your life out there. I found your book just in time. I was just about to leave my husband and my children. I just couldn't take it anymore. When I read your book, I discovered that I was partly at fault for all of the dysfunction in my home. Thank you again for saving my marriage."

—Sandra

"I thought my husband was a jerk, that my marriage was dull, and that I should have married someone else. . . .When I read your book, I discovered I was married to a real winner. I never realized how lucky I am. Nobody is perfect, including me, but I so appreciate the husband I have."

FOREWORD

Wisdom is not the sole purview of academia, and workable marriage counseling strategies are not exclusively found in textbooks. In Helper, Utah, sage wisdom can be found at the Risqué Beauty Salon. The most powerful yet pragmatic marriage counseling tools that I have ever used in my clinical practice were the books written by Sherri Mills, the proprietor of the Risqué. Sherri's book, *Marriage 101 for Men: Why Taking Out the Trash is a Turn-On,* provides real-world solutions to issues that sabotage marital accord, and is written in such a manner as to make sense to the male partner in a marriage.

Sherri's creation rationally ties the shared responsibility of managing a home to an improved sex life. The book does not condemn men for their lack of sensitivity and domestic motivation but outlines how to educate men in such matters. A clear picture of what divorce is and is not (a guarantee of happiness) is presented, and instructions on developing family contracts (a technique I have adopted) are given in an easy-to-understand format.

Marriage 101 for Men is a must-have for marriage and family counselors and a must-read for couples experiencing marital discord. As is the case with this author's first book, *I Almost Divorced My Husband, but I Went on Strike Instead,* I shall make *Marriage 101 for Men* a must-read for all of the male premarriage and marriage counseling clients with whom I work. (This book is a great handbook for those who are about to marry.)

With Respect,
Karl F. Kraync, MS, CRC, NCC, LPC
(I am an old warrior with forty-four years of counseling experience)

ACKNOWLEDGMENTS

To my husband, Gerald, who has never faltered in his support of my projects. You can bet that I never take him for granted. I can see on a daily basis what a lucky gal I am. He is phenomenal.

To my editor Elaine Rhode. I can't say enough about this super intelligent, kind human angel. Our compatibilities are unmatched.

My daughter Nicole, who continues to drop everything she is doing to come to my rescue.

To Hailey, Braidy, and Morgan, who became my computer brain.

To my wonderful grandchildren; they make life worth living. There isn't enough love in the world to shower on these wonderful living gifts. They are Derek, Morgan, Ross, Bodie, Braidy, Hailey, Maegan, Kelsey, Hanna, Nathan, Mark Jr., Carter, Dan, Kyzer, and my wonderful great-grandson, Conner.

To my children, who are still my best friends: Guy and Chanda, Rod and Nancy, and Nicole and Mark.

I need to give a special thanks to my clients. Without them I wouldn't have any stories. My clients trusted me enough to share their pain and vulnerabilities with me. I will always honor their trust. No one will ever know who *they* are.

To John (not his real name, but you know who you are): You were the inspiration for this book. I am so happy that you felt a need for men to have some coaching. Thank you so much for your support and input.

Thank you, Dr. Joshua Coleman, psychologist and author, for allowing me to credit and use your wisdom in important places in this book.

ACKNOWLEDGMENTS

To Bianca Dumas: thank you again for getting me on the path to being a published author. I won't forget it.

To Rodney Fife: I can't thank you enough for always being there and staying on

INTRODUCTION

I n the early months of signings for my first book, *I Almost Divorced my Husband, But I Went on Strike Instead,* I received a challenge from a male reader in an email:

Sherri, you have no idea how many points you make that are right on track. I appreciate all the good things you said about us men—and the benefits of your ideas seem so easy to see. I believe everyone would win. We men really would fight to the death for our women. Like you said, the reeducation process can be painful—but worth it!

The idea of "helping" versus "owning" a job as mine alone opened my eyes. I better understand the frustration my wife felt and the enormous job she did. [Your first] book, however, has a pretty strong focus on women, and it makes it a little tough to digest at times. I understand what you are trying to accomplish, so I "get it." I think some material focused on helping men would be a great addition in future revisions of your [first] book. —John

John, through your encouragement and my publisher's agreement, together we've gone one better—a whole book written specifically for men.

* * *

During my long-ago strike to save my marriage and my sanity, I discovered that men (including my husband) really have no idea the hardships women go through after working a job all day only to come home to another full-time job, one with no time off, no sick leave, and little or no appreciation, understanding, or respect.

My big, strong, manly husband did not cave in to a demanding wife. He started out trying to prove that he could do everything better than I did. He was out to prove that he and the kids didn't need me. After immersing himself in the invisible, repetitive, thankless household tasks that sapped his energy as they had mine, he was horrified. He had no idea what he had inadvertently put me through and was more than happy to make my life better—permanently.

I wrote this and my first book because, more than twenty years later, relationships throughout our nation are still not equal—despite the simple solution. After interviewing more men, women, children, and numerous psychologists, I sadly realized that the dynamics haven't changed much at all.

I wrote these books because I have seen too many divorces that didn't have to happen. Yes, divorces happen for many reasons, but more marriages could be saved if one or both of the parties didn't come to the table seething with resentment, anger, and eventually pure hate because the couple didn't know how to confront the double standard and double duty of householder work.

Thus my goal is to broadcast the solution to the imbalance of householder work and all its dangerous fallout so that fair division of labor will become commonplace. I want the sharing of chores to be automatic, no longer the ticking time bomb in marriages of our children and grandchildren.

—Sherri Mills

CHAPTER 1

HOUSEWORK—YOUR MISSING LINK TO SEX

I do like hugs and kisses—but what I like more is you doing dishes.

—Author unknown

Let's start with a blunt message that speaks directly to your interests. What you need and what your wife needs. How the two differ and how they can be achieved through the same action on your part.

Initially you may be skeptical about a woman writing this book for your benefit, even though I've studied for more than four decades the marital ups and downs through generations of men and women (and their children) from grassroots America—folks who could be you.

This book will give you the game plan for mastering that surprisingly elusive, permanent win-win solution for both you and your wife: great sex and a great life together.

First, however, I invite you to listen—man to man—to a summary of marital research findings on sex and housework, written by noted psychologist and author Dr. Joshua Coleman.

SEX AND HOUSEWORK

"Sex is a subject that is near and dear to most men's hearts. It's often one of the most important predictors for men's satisfaction in

3

marriage. So why do some men have wives who want to get it on while others don't?

"Marital researcher John Gottman made an interesting discovery: women are more interested in having sex when they're married to men who are more willing to do housework.

Putting her hands on you

"Why would putting your hands into dishwater make your wife more interested in putting her hands on you?

"A good sex life makes men feel important, cared about, and connected with their wives. For women, a good sex life is further down the list below a man's affection, caring, communication, and his interest in the kids and house, according to research by Gottman and E. M. Hetherington and John Kelly. While sex is in the female gumbo of marital satisfaction, it ain't the main ingredient.

Big turn-off to treat wife as servant

"As Gottman writes in *Why Marriages Succeed or Fail*, 'Housework may seem like a trivial concern compared to sexuality, but women see it as a major issue affecting their sex life. Treating your wife as a servant will almost inevitably affect the more intimate, fragile parts of a relationship. Being the sole person to clean the toilet is definitely not an aphrodisiac.'

"Why the difference between the genders? Because sex isn't scarce for women. Almost any woman could walk out the door and find a guy to have sex with her within a matter of hours. She may not love the choices, but she wouldn't have much problem making it happen.

What's scarce for women?

"What's scarce for women isn't a man who's willing to have sex— it's a man who's willing to help raise children, do housework, talk about his feelings, and be affectionate.

"Therefore, when a guy does housework it has several effects on a woman's sexuality. The first is that it makes her feel cared about. It's a way of saying, 'No, you're not in this marriage to serve me and clean up after me. I'm not going to dump everything on you. I care enough about you to do my share.'

Stress reduces women's sex drive

"This is important to a woman's desire because *it decreases her stress levels.* Women's sexual interest is tied to stress for evolutionary reasons. Since women only ovulate once a month, they have a very finite number of opportunities to spread their genes over the course of their lifetimes. They are right to be more conservative about choosing a man who will increase the likelihood of those offspring surviving.

You know this part

"Men, theoretically, can spread their genes on a daily basis. Therefore, from an evolutionary perspective, men worry less about their offspring surviving and more about maximizing the opportunities to spread their genes. So men's sexual interest isn't bothered by such trivial distractions as mood, energy level, stress, or whether or not we even like the person—whereas for women, these concerns are typically more central.

Your first action—not Victoria's Secret

"The moral of this story is that if you feel dissatisfied with how little your wife wants to have sex with you, the first action isn't to purchase something from the Victoria's Secret catalogue; it's to look at your feelings about the toilet bowl."

(Excerpt from Dr. Joshua Coleman's The Lazy Husband)[1]

* * *

Sex and housework, undoubtedly a most unlikely pairing of topics in your mind! But, as you've just read in the message from professional researchers and as is underscored in the rest of my book, they are vitally linked if you want to achieve your highest marital satisfaction. Trust me. I know. Read on!

NOTES

1. Joshua Coleman, *The Lazy Husband: How to Get Men to Do More Parenting and Housework* (New York: St. Martin's Press, 2005).

CHAPTER 2

IS THIS HOW YOUR MARRIAGE HAS GONE?

They shared the chores of living as some couples do.
She did most of the work—he appreciated it too.

—Paula Gosling

You just got married. Everything is wonderful. You have a beautiful wife with sparkling personality. You are very much in love. You have a good job. Your wife has a good job too, which helps in this economy.

Your wife is a good cook. She keeps the house clean. You have a fantastic sex life. You both have so much fun together. You can't wait until the day is over so you can go home and be with your wife.

THINGS, THEY ARE A CHANGIN'

After a while, however, on weekends she seems to be busy doing other things, so you go fishing with a buddy. You come home; she is still busy. So you park yourself in front of the TV and watch a ball game or two.

Gradually you have little spats over things that shouldn't really mean much. (Unknown to you, your wife is beginning to resent all of your free time while she has little.)

You are happy. You have a beautiful wife, a mostly good sex life, and a nice home. You don't see the lopsided workload because life is as it should be, according to what you and your wife have been taught by society.

In a 2010 keynote address to the Renfrew Center Foundation, women's movement icon Gloria Steinem addressed the myth fed to us by society that women can work full-time jobs and take sole charge of a household and children, all while maintaining their figures and social lives. "Women are told they can have it all, that they can do anything, as long as they keep doing everything else they were doing before," Steinem said. And when they find, after all, that they can't do it all, they don't know how to approach the subject with their husbands and ultimately end up feeling like failures. "We're women. We were trained to be nice," says Steinem about speaking out for equality. "We [aren't] direct enough."[1]

THINKING, BUT NOT SAYING

Your wife thinks, if she waits long enough, that you—being the wonderful husband that you are—will help her with household tasks because you love her. When you don't, your wife thinks you couldn't love her or you would realize how unfair her workload is.

You can't read her mind. You already do your part—your full-time job, as society says, is your role. And referring to Gloria Steinem's statement, society and your upbringing say that your wife is responsible for the rest, whether or not she works outside the home. You are thinking, "All she has to do is make the beds, cook, and do dishes. How hard can that be?"

I remember a time when my children were all home and we were all getting ready to go somewhere. My oldest son became irritated and asked me what was taking me so long.

I said, "I just have to finish cleaning the kitchen, vacuum, and make my bed, then I will be ready."

His answer was, "I could do all of that in five minutes."

The crazy thing about it was that I really believe that he thought he could.

IS SHE BECOMING BORING?

You don't tell your wife that you are beginning to think she is a little boring. When you want to do something fun together, her excuses are more frequent. She says she loves you, but after working all week, she only has the weekend to keep up with the housework.

SHE FEELS GUILTY / ANGRY

Once in a while, your wife asks you to help. But unknown to you (and sometimes to her) she feels guilty because, subconsciously or consciously, she thinks it is her job to keep up everything on the home front. She has been taught by her parents and everyone around her that it is her responsibility, and even advertisements and movies portray that fact.

Maybe you try to help. Wash the dishes. Take out the trash. Mow the lawn. You can't figure out why she can't find time to do anything fun when you always do. It takes her way too long to get her stuff done and then get ready.

WILL BABY MAKE THINGS BETTER?

Suddenly a baby is on the way. You are both ecstatic. Then your wife gets morning sickness. She is still working at her outside job and at home. Internally your wife is feeling overwhelmed. But she still refuses to (or can't) tell you what is wrong. She thinks you should know. You, the husband, couldn't know, of course. She doesn't tell you, and she and you have been anticipating this new bundle of joy for so long that she doesn't want to rock the boat.

Baby changes

The baby arrives. Your wife gets to stay home from work for a while. You are happy for her. Because she is home all day, she will have so much free time, and all of that time to enjoy the baby. The opposite is true. The time with the baby is all consuming, (but well worth it). However, there is no free time, as you believe.

Sometimes you feel resentful because your wife asks you to help with the dishes or a meal. After all, she is home all day while you work. Add to that, you even change the baby's diapers once in a while. You have also gotten up with the baby during the night at times to help her out. All while you have a full-time job. You think, *"If I have to help, then maybe she is not up to being a mother"* because that is what you have learned from your upbringing and society at large.

NOTE TO GUYS: THIS IS NORMAL! Before you read further, I want to stress emphatically that all this stuff is NORMAL. The fault lies with the wife who won't speak up and our culture/society that makes her feel so guilty that she thinks she's a failure when she can't "do it all."

There is no way that you, the husband, should automatically know that there is a problem. Especially when the evolution is so slow from a happy wife to fed-up wife. You can't realize the monstrous job she has shouldered.

YOU GO OUT, SHE STAYS HOME

You have already mapped out your free time, often with your wife's permission ("Oh honey, you work so hard, you need a break"). Your wife, however, feels more angry and bitter than ever that she doesn't have any free time. But now there is a difference:

Your wife no longer hides her anger. She feels so overloaded and exhausted that her resentment overflows.

The idea that a wife should be able to "do it all" is imbedded in her psyche BY SOCIETY. So once again you get the blame because your wife thinks you should automatically know her predicament and ride to the rescue.

CINDERELLA AT THE STOVE

Now, not only do you sometimes think that your wife is boring (because she never wants to do the things you two used to do together), but you are also noticing that she isn't as attractive as she used to be. If your wife would communicate her situation, she would explain that she is so busy with the baby and house that she has no time for herself.

TRAJECTORY FOR MUTUAL DISAPPOINTMENT

Sometimes your wife's anger blows up into a big scene. You ask her what's wrong, but she only replies, "Nothing." She apologizes later for her outburst. This makes you wonder even more what the big deal is.

You have developed a pattern of coming home from work and either watching TV or going fishing, golfing, working on hobbies, or just riding around with your friends. Really, there isn't much else to do because you have no idea what it takes to run a household and take care of a baby. Your wife hasn't told you. And without doing it 24/7 yourself, you couldn't know.

HELPING OUT A LOT

You are a good husband, so you wash the dishes once in a while, take out the garbage, and sometimes you even change the diaper without being asked.

You are rightfully proud of yourself. You have been helping out a lot. You have been doing more than society really expects of you. But your wife is still fuming. She is perpetually exhausted. She can't believe you don't help her more.

What the heck is going on?

You have no idea you are doing anything wrong. You are beginning to get tired of her attitude. You can't believe that she is still making excuses as to why she never wants to do anything fun.

Your family begins to grow and by now your wife's pattern of never saying anything to you has solidified. You can tell, however, by her body language that she is angry all the time. You just never know why. You ask her what's wrong, but she still replies, "Nothing." You tend to think there might be something wrong with her.

Sexual frustration

Your sex life has dwindled because of her exhaustion and resentment. You are still in the dark about what is wrong. When you ask, your wife repeats that nothing is wrong. But she does know what is wrong. And blames you for not knowing. She can't fix it because she doesn't know how and deep down she still believes all of this extra household stuff is her responsibility and society helps her to keep believing it.

> NOTE TO GUYS: Some couples don't sink into such unhappiness and dysfunction, but some marriages go through far worse and explode in divorce that didn't need to happen. Lack of communication causes havoc in every aspect of a relationship.

Society and upbringing seldom prepare men for the realities of a true partnership. It is not the husband's fault. But that doesn't let you off the hook.

RIDE TO HER RESCUE

You were once the superhero or knight in shining armor to the woman who fell in love with you. You can ride to her rescue again. Indeed, the mutual disappointment and anger described in this chapter can be eliminated.

For both sides it can be eliminated by a strategy where you and your wife together pitch in to balance the load of household chores so that both of you can enjoy time off, time with the children, and—most important—time with each other.

REMINDERS:

- Society has imbedded in our psyche that women should "do it all." This upbringing tosses ticking bombs into today's relationships.

- Often when your wife is angry, she won't say why. She thinks you should read her mind. Agree to communicate *now*, not wait for a crisis. (*see chapters 12 and 13*)

- Start (or restart) your married life sharing household responsibilities and become her hero again. (*see following chapters for tools*)

NOTES

1. Gloria Steinem in Joann Loviglo, "Steinem: Notion of Women 'Having It All' Is a Myth," *Star Tribune*, November 12, 2010.

CHAPTER 3

MORE TIME FOR LOVE

The old saying "women's work is never done" needs updating:
"Reward for shared householder work—more time for love."

The biggest cause of preventable divorce—or unhappiness in marriage—is the imbalance of householder tasks. I call it "householder" work because everyone in the household should carry an equal amount of the burden. And children after a certain age should share in that work to prepare them for their own adult lives and marriages.

HOUSEHOLDER IMBALANCE

I went on strike in our household after trying for years to awaken my Mr. Clueless to how debilitating my "doing it all" had become with three kids and a full-time job.

Perhaps I was at fault. I had set myself up as the woman who did everything, and as the woman, everyone needed me at every minute during the day.

Like an idiot, I had established the routine of getting Gerald's breakfast on the table before I went to work at five or five thirty in the morning. When the children came along, still trying to be the super woman, I continued to get up early and fix a hot breakfast for all. The kids would just move their food around their plates more than they'd eat it, and I'd end up feeding the food to the dog.

MY STRIKE AND THE ORIGIN OF THE CONTRACT

I tried so many schemes to help him see what I was going through, but none of them even made an impression on this relaxed, carefree man who—without being aware of it—I had inadvertently helped to create.

I finally came to the conclusion that the only way to reach him was to deal with him on a level he would understand.

Gerald worked in the office of a clothing factory, where most of the other employees were members of a union. So he dealt with union contracts on a regular basis. I decided that *I* needed a contract that would protect *me* from company abuse. If you think about it, a housewife has the same type of job as a union employee: she does physical labor. She also does it without any of the benefits or pay, and with a lot more responsibility and higher expectations. This is also a job where an employer (call him "husband") hires an employee (call her "wife"), whose job initially appears to be a fairly easy one. Then as the wife comes to the startling realization that this position was not only monstrously more than she bargained for, she also realizes that it provides very few benefits like free time, coffee breaks, or vacation hours. The normal thing to do in this situation would be to abruptly quit and get a job that can be done in eight hours and pays well.

But there's a problem.

She's signed a contract (the marriage contract) and has other obstacles (love and children). So the wife does the next best thing to quitting. She goes to her boss and explains that the position she's in was not explained to her beforehand. Furthermore, she says, in order to do it properly, she needs help.

WALK A MILE IN HER SHOES

But because the husband hasn't been in her shoes yet, he has absolutely no concept of the extent of her responsibilities. They had never been explained to him, either. He is, in fact, still carrying around preconceived notions of what this easy job of housewifery is supposed to be, and he thinks she's crazy and totally inept.

She tries other ways of convincing him that she needs help, but to no avail.

MY STRIKE PREPARATIONS

I realized that we had a problem in our marriage from the very beginning, but I put my problem away and worked at raising my kids. But when my children started school, I finally had time to think. I thought and thought and thought. And woe to the husband who isn't used to a wife who thinks and then who wakes up one day to find a wife who has thought too much.

"Is this all there is?" I wondered. "Is this what I'm going to be doing for the rest of my life?"

No way!

The only thing I could do was come up with a foolproof plan to change things, because it would either be that or a divorce. So I came up with a plan: I went on strike. It was the hardest thing I have ever done, but the payoff is continuing every day. I have my original husband, who is now an angel. My children got to live with their own father, and my grandchildren have the best grandpa anyone could ever ask for.

Some of my best friends and clients were in the same boat but didn't go on strike and are now divorced and forced to deal with step-families. Ironically, those women are still doing it all.

A plan in language a man understands

Using a union contract as a guide, I began writing my marriage and householder contract (*now called a Fair Marriage Contract, Appendix A*). I knew one thing for certain: Gerald understood union contracts. He knew that workers used a contract as a negotiating tool and that if they didn't get at least some of the compensations they wanted in the negotiations, then the workers would go on strike. That was my plan.

I had been negotiating for thirteen years to no avail, so a strike was inevitable—Gerald would actually understand that once I put it in front of him. I had to be ready to go on strike, professionally and calmly, in the way that Gerald was used to workers doing in the company. Before I went on strike, though, I had to have my contract completely prepared. I also had to prepare myself mentally to be able to go through with it no matter what.

I went on strike—eight days of staying strong

The day came. I will remember it forever. I had sent the children to the store to get some things I needed for dinner while I was busy with daily chores, the busyness magnified because it was my only day off. The store was only a couple of blocks away, so it shouldn't have taken the boys any time at all to get there and back. Well, about forty-five minutes later they came sauntering in, discarding the grocery sack on the table, and going on their way. As I peered into the paper sack and immediately noticed the wrong contents. I stopped both of them in their tracks. I demanded to know why they bought the wrong items and why something so easy had taken so long.

Dad to the defense

As usual, Gerald immediately jumped to their defense. "If it's so important for you to get the exact thing," he said, "you ought to get it yourself instead of having the kids *do your job.*"

I could feel the anger seething through my body. This was the moment that made up my mind. *This is the time*, I thought. I now had the reassurance that no matter what happened, my strike would go into effect, and I would never give up.

It was obvious: I was married to a handsome, well-rounded man who made me laugh daily. He was a playful father who adored his children, was the life of the party when we were out with our friends, he was a person who never missed work, was very dedicated to his family, and was a super . . . male chauvinist.

My strike ultimatum

I abruptly ceased anything I was doing, including finishing the cooking I had started. I left the mess that the half-finished supper had splattered all over the kitchen and stated very firmly, "Not only am I not going to the store, but as of this very second, I am officially on strike and don't intend to do anything."

Gerald started to laugh. "Oh," he said with a half-sneer, half-chuckle. "And how do you propose to do that?"

"I have it all written out," I said, calmly but resolutely. "And we don't need to discuss it any further because every possible answer to any questions you have will be found in the file at the beauty salon along with the contract."

What made him go get the contract

I think it was curiosity more than anything that made Gerald get in the car and go down to the salon.

He was gone for what seemed like an eternity.

Planning my strategy

While he was gone I was visualizing how bad the house would look for the entire duration of the strike. I had secretly decided to keep everything picked up on the landing by the front door so visitors would not immediately be aware of the disarray. I also planned to lock myself in the bathroom so I could keep the toilet clean. I knew my husband and children wouldn't notice I had scrubbed the toilet because everybody thought the tooth fairy did that job anyway.

There was a perfect silence in the house. My children's eyes were asking all sorts of questions, but not a word was spoken.

Surprise!

When Gerald finally came home, there was more silence. I was glued to the couch, pretending to watch TV, and all I could hear in the kitchen were the clanging of pans and the clattering of someone setting the table. I was dumbstruck by what had just taken place, and I was a nervous wreck waiting to see what would happen next.

"Daddy said to come and eat," my daughter said.

Stay focused—don't give in to gestures

I slowly walked out to the kitchen and was greeted by a beautifully set table, napkins in place, and my three children sitting in their places, not daring to speak. Pork chops, mashed potatoes, and a beautiful salad adorned the table. There was even pudding for dessert, and the mess from cooking was all cleaned up. Millions of thoughts were rushing through my head, and the first thing I actually wanted to do was to go up and give Gerald a hug, tell him I loved him, and say everything was okay.

I knew I couldn't. I had been here before. Gerald never meant to say or do anything to make things hard for me. I knew that. Besides, he had the personality that could charm the feathers right off a chicken. Inside I was trying to melt, but my head took charge, and I walked back to the TV after supper. It felt like walking a mile with cement in my shoes.

What is going on in his head

I don't know what was going on in Gerald's mind, but the silence was still deafening. I was thinking that he was probably seething inside. But I knew if I gave in now, everything would go back to the way it was in a few short days. I kept telling myself, "You've got to keep going. All your work cannot be for nothing." The most inspirational thing I repeated to myself was, "He will be worth the effort."

DAY TWO

Filled with anticipation, I didn't sleep that night: what would the next day bring?

To my surprise, the same thing happened. Gerald fixed breakfast and enlisted the kids to help clean up. They all went through the house, vacuuming and making beds. When Gerald came from work, he started supper again. I was in perpetual shock. I had prepared for a mess, but not for this. The hardest thing I had to do was to get up from the table after eating a fantastic meal (far better than I would have cooked) and make that long trip back to the couch. I spent the whole time there, not lifting a finger for any reason except to go to the salon. I didn't answer any of the children's questions and told them to call their dad if they had a problem.

Storm brewing—stay calm

On the third day of the strike, I knew something was afoot because first my son Guy sidled past the door, peered in, then went on his way hurriedly like he was getting out of the way. Then my daughter Nicole stood by the door as if to warn me of something, and then I could hear . . . loud stomping footsteps coming up the stairs.

"If you think for one minute that you are going to tell me what to do, you're crazy," Gerald bellowed. He was angrier than I had seen him in a long time. I don't remember the rest of the tirade because I was busy talking to myself in my head. *Hang in there*, I told myself, *He's worth it.*

I kept reminding myself not to get angry back at him. *I can't get mad. I must stay strong. It's almost over. You've come this far. He's worth all the trouble.* The sounds in my head were even louder than Gerald's voice.

Stay calm

I must have internalized my intention not to get angry, because I very calmly stated that I had worked on my strike way too long to allow it to fail. I let him know that, no matter what, I would never quit. I told him about my backup plans and saw the shock on his face, especially when I mentioned making signs and marching up and down the street. In truth, I would have been equally horrified if I had needed to carry out my marching plan. Such a protest wasn't like me, but he knew I meant it.

My bottom line remained solid: staying with this man for a lifetime was certainly worth the effort. I repeated to him that this was my ultimate reason for the strike and the contract.

I reminded him of his friends whose wives had asked their husbands for help. These men had refused and had found themselves in divorce court. I let him know that I had the man I wanted and was willing to do whatever it took to keep him.

Hang in there for sincerity!

After that, Gerald actually wanted to sign the contract, but he would certainly have been doing it insincerely.

I insisted the contract was not going to be signed until I was certain that Gerald had read the whole thing and understood it completely. I could tell by his attitude that he just wanted to get me off his back. He wasn't at all sincere. He hadn't even read the whole contract, and all my work would have been for nothing if I had let him sign it—he wouldn't have committed to the division of labor I'd proposed. The contract wasn't a legal document, so I couldn't actually force him to do anything he signed up for, and we would have had to struggle all over again.

CHILDREN NEED REEDUCATING TOO

The only way the contract could work was that after he read the whole contract and empathetically understood it, he would have to meet with the kids and explain to them what their part was. I had allowed them to skip out on all householder work just as I had their father, and that had to be remedied too. Only then would we negotiate.

Children's reaction

Although the children were stunned and curious most of the time, all three had their combative moments.

Nicole came up to me one day and quite nastily stated, "I can't believe what you're making dad do. How would you like to do it all plus go to work?" *Well, duh,* I thought.

Then Rod took his turn. "Lanny Turner said you're stupid for going on strike."

I patted his head and asked very firmly, "Do you really want to know what I think about what Lanny Turner is saying?"

Guy was the oldest and was extremely embarrassed and just leered at me a lot.

Breakthrough

After a little over a week of coming home from work and then taking care of everything at home, Gerald came to me and said, "Tell the kids to be here when I get home." Very compassionately he continued, "We need to change some things. Have the contract ready."

"Are you sure?" I asked. I felt in that moment that I loved him more than was possible. "I bet you're exhausted."

"I am," Gerald said. "But the sad thing about all of this is, you have done it all along."

When the kids were home, Gerald sat them down at the table and I brought out the contract. We divided fifty-two chores among two adults and three children. Gerald would be totally responsible for the basement, outdoor chores, lawn, garbage, and garage. If he got home from work first, he would fix dinner. The children took on the responsibility for doing their own laundry, cleaning their rooms, and doing one extra chore. We even divided the vacation chores right then and there. Everyone signed the contract, and we ended with tears and a big hug.

He understood

The first thing I remember happening after the strike was Rod running up the stairs and demanding, "Mom, where is my blue shirt? I need it today!"

Gerald wasted no time getting to the top of the steps, putting his finger in Rod's face, and answering, "Do you realize your mom has her own clothes to keep track of? She hasn't got time to keep track of four more peoples' clothes. Now, you go and find your own shirt."

I just about fell over with happiness.

NOW I WAS ON VACATION TOO

Vacations changed too. Our family has always loved to go camping, but I used to be the one who packed, did all the cooking and cleaning during the camping trip, and unpacked and cleaned again when we arrived home. But the first camping trip after the strike was different. Gerald instructed the kids to pack their own clothes before we left. He and the kids helped me pack the trailer and prepare the food. Then, at that beautiful, green mountain campsite, Gerald took on the role of chief cook. On the drive home, he reminded everyone what they were supposed to bring in from the truck or trailer, so that we all had an equal amount of work to do.

AN AWAKENING FOR BOTH OF US

It was through my own transition from an overworked and angry wife to a fairly-worked and happy wife that I came to the startling conclusion that men don't put their wives in this terrible position on purpose. Nor did Gerald cave in and become whipped by a striking wife.

My strong, masculine man started out the strike trying to prove he could do everything better than I had, and ultimately realized what a monstrous endeavor it was. When he realized what I put up with day after day, he was horrified and even wanted to change the situation for me. In fact, *he never even knew I was suffering* until I let him experience my workload for himself.

HONEYMOON RESULTS EVERY DAY

When my husband experienced my crazy-making workload for himself, he was appalled and quick to make permanent changes.

What happened next was even beyond both our wildest hopes. We were newlyweds again! We enjoyed great bedtimes, great spontaneous travel and play, and a loving, nag-free atmosphere.

MY HUSBAND'S STORY

When my strike and its results got media attention, Gerald (my husband) told a reporter the following:

Never gave two hoots

"I used to listen to my wife's complaints of having too much to do, but I never gave two hoots. I was spoiled. I grew up thinking the woman had her place and the guy had his. Housework was women's work and all of that. But I can see now that that's a bad situation."

I figured I would win

"It never really hit me in the face until Sherri brought that fair marriage contract out [at the start of her strike] and stopped doing everything for me and the kids. I wasn't going to sign her contract," he said. "I figured I would wear her down. I figured I would win; I would show her we didn't need her any more. I was going to play it to the end.

Now I understood in my gut

"Then I had to do 'everything' for the duration of her eight-day strike—seemed like a year—and I understood in my gut what she had been going through all during our marriage. What I had taken for granted.

"Now I feel good about taking my share of householder responsibilities," he said. "We're a lot closer since 'the strike.' I feel good because Sherri feels good."

We really share our marriage

The reporter heard Sherri quietly singing the tune: "When mama ain't happy, ain't nobody happy." She told the reporter, "I now have time to look nice for Gerald, and I feel more rested for the first time in years. I know to the core that we really share our marriage."

REWARDS KEEP COMING

The continuing rewards from our division of labor keep us grinning—and loving.

Gerald says doing his share of householder tasks is a small price to pay for not having his wife (me) mad at him all the time. We suddenly had more time together, more mutual respect, more compatibility on how to discipline the children, and, of course, a better sex life.

HOW GOOD THIS FEELS!

On one of Gerald's business trips to San Francisco, we were relaxing on the bed of our luxurious hotel room before going out to dinner and a night on the town with Gerald's colleagues.

"Do you realize this is the first of all our trips to San Francisco you haven't been so exhausted we couldn't have fun?" Gerald said. He hugged me tightly. "You don't know how good this feels."

FAMILIAR BACK STORY

Prior to my family sharing household tasks, I would work myself to exhaustion before traveling with Gerald. I would be dog-tired on the trip and ruin everyone's fun by insisting on ending the evening early. Gerald actually started to wait until the last minute to let me know about a trip so I wouldn't go gangbusters on the house. It didn't work. I would stay up all night if I had to.

After we shared the workload, we couldn't believe how much fun we could have together on trips when I stopped being catatonic!

* * *

HE NEVER KNEW

My strong, masculine man started out the strike trying to prove he could do everything better than I had, and ultimately realized what a monstrous endeavor it was. When he realized what I put up with day after day, he was horrified and wanted to change the situation for me. In fact, *he never even knew I was suffering* until I let him experience my workload for himself.

MEN ARE NOT AT FAULT

Let me say that again, loudly. Men are not at fault. I wrote my first book (and now this book) because, through the process of going on strike, I discovered that the majority of women's frustrations with marriage are not your fault. I know! Most wives blame their husbands as if it is their fault. Their anger and resentment are definitely directed toward the wrong target. Come hell or high water, I want to correct that delusion. Men who read my first book asked me to write one for them. Here it is.

REMINDERS:

- The biggest cause of preventable divorce—or unhappiness in marriage—is the imbalance of householder tasks

- Although anger and resentment from a wife is warranted, it's mostly directed at the wrong person. Men are not at fault.

CHAPTER 4

MEN ARE NOT AT FAULT, BUT YOU'RE NOT OFF THE HOOK

You can ride to her rescue
like a superhero or knight in shining armor
to make your marriage all you ever hoped it would be.

Knowing what I know now, I can't even imagine my loving husband Gerald putting up with me as long as he did before my life-changing strike. I inadvertently helped to create the very behavior I was railing against by shouldering all the householder tasks myself and letting my husband, and then our children, skate free. I reinforced their carefree behavior for the first twelve years of our marriage, even while I desperately tried to change things. I definitely wasn't a very fun person—a complainer, a whiner, a resentful person who was angry most of the time.

It's no surprise that lopsided householder responsibilities trigger such negative reactions. The results may be predictable, but husbands aren't aware of what is wrong because (1) society and wives try to mask the problem, and (2) they don't know how to fix the imbalance.

DECADES OF LISTENING
TO REAL-LIFE MARITAL PROBLEMS

Over the course of my career, I have heard decades of real-life marital problems and real-life outcomes, successes, and failures. I've had weekly and monthly sessions with my clients, over periods of years or lifetimes. I have the advantage over professional counselors of sticking with clients through generations, so I see more than the immediate result of a divorce. I see them after their quick fixes have turned into nightmare rides, and all the while their children are hooked to the tailgate.

"RESEARCH ON LIFE" CHANGES MY LIFE

I spent the first part of my hairdressing career listening to clients' problems but keeping my big mouth shut. Sometimes I offered support, and I always kept their confidence.

After a few years of consistently cutting my clients' hair, I knew the pros and cons of every choice they'd make. I called it my "research on life." This increased my interest in relationships and personal growth, and I began a massive research campaign to read everything I could about these subjects, a passion I still exercise today. It became easier for me to know what to say to my clients when they asked for advice, because I knew what results they might have.

DIVORCE NOT AN OPTION FOR ME

I always felt fortunate to see the consequences of my clients' divorces, and the lessons I learned became one of the reasons I decided not to file for divorce during the low points of my marriage. Over and over again I saw too many dream solutions turn into nightmares. I knew that divorce would not be an option for me. I'll tell you why:

COMMON-SENSE REASONS NOT TO DIVORCE

(1) When a couple hasn't learned how to fix the problem of overwork in their first marriage, the chance of having the same situation crop up in a subsequent marriage is enormous.

(2) After divorce, the original husband and wife both have to navigate their children's relationship with stepparents. Sometimes those relationships work out. Very often they don't.

(3) If you have a good woman who simply adores her children,

it seems like a no-brainer to keep her and work your heart out to fix whatever is wrong.

FAMILIES WITH CHILDREN AT RISK

Now I want you (and the world) to know that before you pull the plug on your marriage, there are many alternatives. I have *rarely* seen a family with young children find a better life after divorce, except the case of abuse.

Most divorced couples experience the same disappointments they had before divorce, except that shortly after a second marriage they also have to deal with stepparenting and jealousy from the new spouse. My heart breaks for the children who have to live between parents whose relationship has fallen apart. These children are my clients too, and I hear about their suffering firsthand.

GOAL

My hope is to somehow reach men in relationships that haven't fallen apart yet. There are ways to heal a relationship, providing it is free from physical or emotional abuse. The love can be brought back when unacknowledged problems are brought to the surface and worked on in the right way.

Easier than you think

In this book, I am going to give you tools for making your married life filled with masculine pride and pleasure for yourself and easier and more loving for your wife.

You'll experience positive changes even as you start making a slight effort.

Fight the disrespect she perceives

It's not so much about all the extra work your wife has to do that makes her angry and resentful. It is the disrespect she perceives—that you take for granted she must "do it all" (and yet you have no concept of the enormous cumulative time and energy "doing it all" entails). On top of the disrespect she feels, the icing on the cake (*emphasis on ICE!*) is when you ignore her exhaustion and expect her to be ready to go places or to jump in the sack at a moment's notice.

Newlyweds and fiancés can do it "right" from the start

Sharing householder tasks will be easier for men who are newly-weds or who are about to be married.

Jump-start sharing

Nevertheless, you may need to be proactive and strong here. Don't let your lovely lady's exhilaration and pride fool you (or her!) into thinking she is going to have time and energy to be waiting on you hand and foot in the years to come. Begin your marriage waiting on each other.

Think like a buddy

When you first decide to get married, both of you can sit down and choose which areas in the house you each are best suited for. (If it helps, pretend you are moving in with a buddy. Don't expect anything from your spouse that you wouldn't expect from a buddy.) Decide right then to divide the currently known responsibilities and those that come up in the future.

Intimate rewards

That way, when your first child comes on the scene, you will know instinctively to share the chores and ultimately the tremendous joy that comes from having your children and helping them grow.

When two people are cooperating on the home front, you will be amazed how much more intimacy can blossom and thrive.

REMINDERS:

- Husbands are in the dark because society and wives mask the problem.

- It's not so much the extra work that causes the anger and resentment—it's the disrespect she perceives.

- When you first get married, pretend you're moving in with a buddy. Don't expect anything from your wife that you wouldn't expect from a buddy in household duties.

CHAPTER 5

PREVENTABLE DIVORCES:
Two Examples

It's a nightmare ride—with children hooked to the tailgate.

C ouples are on a collision course when one person is deliriously happy and the other is seething inside. Both husband and wife suffer immensely when they go through a divorce. It's a nightmare ride—with children hooked to the tailgate. Far better to work to keep your first love your last love and your family together.

Case Study #1

Bottom line: Lack of communications rips a happily married couple apart—because a wife's unspoken resentments over the imbalance of householder tasks weren't addressed as they happened (and, honestly, no husband is a mind-reader). Too late, each wish they had worked to fix their relationship.

Case Study #2

Bottom line: A simple action like sharing household chores can be the catalyst that saves marriages (and children) from divorces that didn't have to happen.

CASE STUDY #1: LACK OF COMMUNICATION WREAKS HAVOC

Jim was thrust into immobilizing shock. His wife, Helen, had just served him with divorce papers. In his mind, he had a great marriage and had been a wonderful father. He worshiped his children. He worked hard to support his family. He loved his wife and kids, and together they had a lot of fun. He could think of nothing he could have done differently and wondered what kind of insanity could have gripped Helen.

Wonderful marriage

Jim looked back on his life with such fondness. He had married the love of his life. Their marriage seemed perfect. He was the sole breadwinner and he figured it was kind of him to let Helen stay home with the kids when they came along. In his mind, he couldn't have had a better life or a better wife. He would go to work and come home to a hot meal every day after work. She made his lunches and sometimes put little notes in his lunch box, telling him how much she loved him. When he went golfing, hunting, or fishing on the weekend, she was always there to feed him when he got home. How much better could it be?

Resentment simmering

Through Helen's eyes, her life was different: She was at Jim's beck and call twenty-four hours a day, seven days a week. Contrast that with Jim who worked eight hours a day, five days a week. Helen didn't voice her disappointment. But deep down she had been seething for years. She had been doing all the domestic work alone for so long—from laundry to paying bills to weeding the flower beds and getting the kids to all their appointments—that the love she had once felt for Jim was now a distant memory. In fact, Helen told me she never had loved Jim.

The truth

I was there in the beginning of their courtship and marriage, so I knew how much Helen did love Jim, and how much they loved each other. But I also knew the intense resentment she toted around with her daily. It was easy for me, seeing her overworked for years, to understand how she could forget her love. Helen's denial that she had ever loved Jim eased her guilt and made it easier to explain to people why she was taking her children's father away from them.

Helen had told me everything. I have been a hairdresser for forty years and had been hers for a decade. And as you know, people tell their hairdressers everything.

I wondered if Helen had ever told Jim how overloaded she felt? Or if she had, what had prevented him from hearing her and helping to make it better?

In the ensuing days, weeks, and months, I heard both sides of their story. They were both my clients. I had cut their hair for years, and it seemed both couldn't wait to talk to me.

Jim's reality

One Friday, Jim came in. I had made sure when he made his appointment that the salon would be empty so he could talk freely if he wanted to, and boy, did he want to. "She always said she was happy," he told me. "She always told me she loved me and was always doing things for me." This statement sent a jolt to my gut. I knew how resentful she was for doing all those things, and he had taken it as a sign of her love.

A few disappointments of his own

"What things did you do for her?" I asked.

"I do everything!" Jim snapped back so quickly that I knew he must have had a few disappointments of his own. "I do everything for her. I work hard to support her and the kids. I bought her a coat for her birthday." He listed a few more twice-yearly good deeds.

What he said next was telling.

He said, "I don't know why she is so upset. I let her stay home all day." Then he added, "What if she had to work like you do and then come home and take care of everything?"

"She never told me"

He got an earful. I said, "Jim, you obviously have no idea what it takes to take care of little kids all day. At least I have adults to talk to during the day." I continued, "In some ways I think her job is probably harder than mine."

I don't think he even heard what I said.

Jim looked at me in the mirror. "She never once told me she was unhappy," he said "How was I to know, until now she'd never mentioned how my fishing and golfing bothered her. Or that she wanted me to help with the house and kids."

Helen's philosophy

I couldn't wait for Helen to come in because she had been complaining profusely to me for years.

"Jim said you never told him any of the things you've told me." I said.

"I never have," Helen said with a shrug. "He should have known."

IF MEN COULD READ MINDS, THEY'D BE IN THE CIRCUS

Men are put in an impossible situation. Your wife and society tell you everything is okay, but too late you find that bogus. Be ever vigilant and don't let this happen to you.

I have seen husbands blind-sided by this situation in case after case. When someone—in this example, the wife—doesn't voice her disappointment early on, that disappointment builds until it explodes into disaster. She found it easier to abandon ship rather than approach her husband and together fix their (relation)ship.

Divorce fallout—his

While shaken and torn from the family he wanted, Jim was in the middle of a thriving career and thought he was financially set. At first he was, but then he began paying child support and paying attorneys to go back to court for trivial things. Gradually his money moved from his account to his attorney's account.

Divorce fallout—hers

Helen, on the other hand, had to work full-time and overtime. Her responsibilities with the children magnified because now she was the sole parent in her household, and her children struggled after the divorce. She couldn't be there for them when they needed her because she was always working. Gone was the attendance at school functions and the hugs and greetings when the kids got home from school. Her children acted as if they had been abandoned and resented Helen for moving them from their big, beautiful home into "the dump" as they called their apartment.

No one like her

Jim was a broken man. He never did get over Helen. He worshiped her. He broke down in tears when he talked to me about her. (This was from a man whom I had never seen show his emotions.) He said he would do anything to get her back.

He said "I'll sell all of my toys, golf clubs, hunting, and fishing gear."

He even said he would do all the housework for the rest of their marriage if he could have her back.

It was too late. Her mind was made up. I didn't have the tools at that time to help them save their marriage. It has haunted me ever since.

Unhappiness all around

Helen's life was no bed of roses. She married twice and told me just recently that it would have been better for the kids and easier for her if she had just stayed.

Jim did marry once more, but that didn't last. He never did get over Helen.

This all happened over twenty years ago. Jim passed away a few years ago. He was alone for the last ten years of his life. He said to me, "I will never find anyone who can hold a candle to Helen."

CHILDREN AND ADULTS SCARRED

What a waste. A happily married couple dissolves into misery— just because resentments weren't addressed as they occurred. We have Helen, who, after two tries, still thinks she was better off with her first love. And we have Jim, who was extremely unhappy for the remainder of his life. We have three children who have never remained close because their loyalties were never in sync as far as their mom and dad were concerned. How much better it would have been if both parents had pitched in to keep their marriage and family together.

CASE STUDY #2: DIVORCE REVERBERATES THROUGH CHILD, SECOND MARRIAGES

Robert and Julie had a beautiful wedding. They were high school sweethearts, high achievers, and came from prominent families in the community. Almost the whole town went to the wedding.

Housework—her job

The marriage seemed okay at first. Their domestic situation, however, was rocky. Most of their fights were about Robert not doing his share of householder duties.

A reprieve came when Justin was born. They were both out of their minds with happiness over this tiny bundle.

Explode into divorce

When Justin was five years old, the marriage exploded. Julie had had enough. Her pride told her anything would be better than the quagmire she found herself in.

Robert found himself alone because Julie got custody of Justin. Robert only got him on Wednesdays and every other weekend.

Using son as weapon

Holidays became nightmares because they both wanted Justin at those times.

Both Julie and Robert tried to buy Justin's love. They both overindulged him. They used him as a weapon to make the other ex miserable. This turned Justin into a troubled kid. He began shoplifting and he was a holy terror in the classroom.

After a few years, Robert remarried and had two additional children.

Stepparents

Robert's new wife, Sophie, had no patience with the spoiled brat Justin had become, and began leaving him out of family gatherings. This made Justin's behavior even worse.

Julie, in time, finally found the (supposed) man of her dreams.

Clark was a divorced father. His son, Dillon, was three years younger than Justin. After a very short honeymoon period, Julie could detect a marked hatred coming from Clark toward Justin.

Son's tailspin

Clark acted like everything was all right as long as Justin was out of the picture. Julie's visits to my salon began and ended with her sobbing and not knowing what to do.

Robert couldn't do much about it. He had to just sit back and watch his son's life deteriorate.

Clark was extremely abusive to his stepson. The Justin-in-trouble situation got increasingly worse, and Justin turned to drugs at a very early age.

More divorces

Julie was at her wits' end, ultimately divorced the ever-increasing abuser she had married.

Justin went on to sell drugs and ended up in jail. Robert, the once proud father, eventually had nothing to do with him.

If only we had worked together

Before her third marriage, Julie sobbed to me, "Sherri, if only I could have swallowed my pride with Robert, and worked on my marriage, everything in my life would have been different." She added that all-too-familiar disappointment: "The only thing that was wrong in our marriage was that he expected me to do everything in the house." She sighed. "Can you imagine how much easier that would have been than my life after Robert?"

She looked like a little old lady sitting before me.

Roberts's marriage to Sophie was destined for failure from the beginning. She obviously didn't like Robert's son and Robert had never learned to be involved in householder duties.

EVERYONE SUFFERS

Both men and women can suffer immensely when they go through a divorce. A simple action like sharing household chores is sometimes the catalyst that can save marriages (and families) from divorces that didn't have to happen.

REMINDERS

- Be alert. Are you like the husband who was clueless to his wife's unhappiness? Clueless to the fact that his life was about to dive off a cliff?

- Address resentments early on, when they are small, and before they explode beyond repair into divorce.

- Simple actions like sharing housework can fix marriages and avoid divorces (and children's backlash) that didn't need to happen.

CHAPTER 6

PART ONE: "HELP" IS A FOUR-LETTER WORD

They shared the chores of living as some couples do.
She did most of the work—he appreciated it too.

—Paula Gosling

H elp" is a favor you do for someone when it's convenient for you or if you feel like doing it.

When you help, the job is *not* your responsibility before and after. Someone else must keep track of what needs to be done, watch deadlines, have tools on hand, ask you for help, and tell you what to do and when to do it.

In a marriage, if these requests for help come repeatedly with lots of directions or criticism, you will call it nagging . . . your wife will call it another job on her already long list.

FIGHTS OVER "HELP" IN MARRIAGE RANK #1

On an episode of *Good Morning America* in 2002, sixteen couples were asked what caused the most contention in their marriages. Surprisingly the answer was not sex, nor money, nor in-laws. The men and women all said the most fights and dissatisfaction arose over husbands somehow not "helping" at home. The women said that if their husbands did "help," they did it poorly and had to be told constantly what to do.

37

"HELP" IS TOO VAGUE

Our society has modernized in almost every area. We got stuck, however, regarding domesticity. One sticky little four-letter word has held us back: HELP.

Throughout the decades, that "help" slowly evolved into a dirty word in marriages, the idea that men should—at minimum—do something in the household arena has become more common. *Marriage counselors and the media often encourage husbands to "help your wife out once in a while."* Although this approach starts to tackle the ingrained societal resistance to wiping out the imbalance of householder tasks, it only throws fuel on a fire waiting to explode.

The well-intentioned but incendiary advice:

- uses the vague word "help"
- asks for far too little
- assumes that all domestic stuff is women's work in the first place

Hey guys, you know that helping a buddy on occasion is relatively uncomplicated. And you undoubtedly also have experienced that helping periodically in a marriage can be a minefield of frustration and discontent on both sides, even though you are trying to be loving.

For example, when your wife says you should help her, what does that mean? Does that mean carry in the groceries? Change the baby's diapers? Clean the bathroom? Does it mean to follow her around and help with everything? Or could it be something in between? At the root of the problem, your wife doesn't know the solution either, short of doing everything herself—which laid the minefield in the first place.

"HELP" ISN'T HELPFUL

The detonator for all these mines—and the reason the solution isn't obvious—is the fact that "help" isn't "help*ful*." It only gives your wife one more job to do regularly. It also provides the ammunition for her to nag you.

The problem is so pervasive, even pop psychology programs such as Dr. Phil point to "help's" minefield. In an episode he asked the couple he was interviewing, "What upsets you most about your partner?"

The man said, "She nags me all the time."

The woman's said, "He does absolutely nothing around the house."

Dr. Phil's answer was that the husband should help his wife more. And that the wife should quit nagging.

What else could he say? He said the right thing. He said the same thing every other psychologist has said. The part that he missed that most professionals still don't know is how to defuse the minefield permanently.

MOUNT EVEREST OF BAGGAGE

If it were the overwork alone on the part of the wife that was causing high divorce rates, the problem would be more easily solved. But resentment, anger, and frustration that come with the work imbalance are far more taxing than physical labor. The Mount Everest of this accumulated baggage is the real reason many women divorce their husbands. It is also the reason that many men are divorcing their wives. Men are tired of being berated on a regular basis.

A leading expert on marriage and relationships, Dr. Joshua Coleman, says it this way: Women resent being in the position of having to ask for help. It forces a wife to beg for something that she feels entitled to have in a shared household. Dr. Coleman says that as a result, some wives manage their resentment by deceiving themselves into thinking that they are more accepting or tolerant of their husband's lack of help than they really are.

His analysis reveals the reason why many wives don't speak up. And why, like lava in a volcano, quiet resentment, frustration, and anger boil on the inside while on the surface your wife seems calm. As you know, duck and cover when her volcano blows![1]

"HELP" ROBS YOU OF YOUR MANHOOD

Help is also good at robbing you of your manhood. Rather than being a gallant gesture of a loving husband, "helping" your wife means that you are at her beck and call. She is the boss.

Who can we blame? Nobody. As author Anna Quindlan wrote, "It's not victim-hood, it's history."

STEP UP TO THE PLATE

Enough is enough! Men are problem solvers. You can fix your home life and marriage—and that of the woman you love.

Instead of accepting and responding to vague, open-ended "help" requests, you can step up to the plate and grab ownership of specific household tasks that will be yours and your alone, daily, weekly, yearly. Your wife will have less on her list of things to do (including bossing!) and more time . . . for you.

(*Go on to Part Two: "Sharing versus Helping—End Nagging"*)

REMINDERS:

- Men not helping at home starts the most marital fights.

- Help is (1) vague; (2) asks far too little; and (3) assumes all domestic stuff is still women's work.

- Help isn't helpful. It only gives your wife one more job to do (figuring out how to get you to help).

- Help robs you of your manhood. Your wife is still the boss.

- Stop saying, "I'll help you." Start saying, "I'll share householder responsibilities."

NOTES

1. Joshua Coleman, *The Lazy Husband: How to Get Men to Do More Parenting and Housework* (New York: St. Martin's Press, 2005).

PART TWO: SHARING VERSUS "HELPING" END NAGGING

Doing nothing is very hard to do. You never know when you are finished.

—Leslie Nielsen

Today we have no logical reason to believe that getting up with children in the middle of the night, changing diapers, washing clothes, buying groceries, cooking dinners, cleaning the cars, ironing, vacuuming, dusting, making beds, mowing lawns, planting flowers, weeding gardens, paying bills, tracking receipts for taxes, washing windows, painting, spackling, wallpapering, making appointments and reservations, packing for trips, unpacking after trips, loading and unloading the dishwasher or washing dishes by hand—along with hundreds of other tasks—are solely women's jobs.

A GOOD HUSBAND?

In the past, our society would award you a good husband rating if you help at home occasionally with some of those above chores when you don't have something more pressing to do.

Attitudes and economics are changing, however. No more is it acceptable for two adults in the house to be working and for only one of them to have a second—or third—job when she gets home. Young women are not putting up with this the way other generations of women did. They are taking the easy way out—getting out. So are men when fighting and nagging overwhelm their lives.

FIX, DON'T LEAVE

Wait! There is an answer, and it's easier than you think. You will be called a great husband, rising far above the *good* rating! Stop struggling with help and step up to sharing responsibilities around the home.

More time together

By shifting your perspective from helping to sharing householder chores, you will free your wife to have fun with you and the kids, to watch sports with you, or to just have the time and energy for a lot more togetherness, especially in the bedroom.

Sharing easier than help

When you select your share of household chores (on a forever basis, just as your wife will), you can do them on your own schedule and in your own way. That fits a man's style better than to be being in the subservient position of waiting to be asked for help and then being told what to do. A request for help usually comes with strings attached: someone else's timing, directions, and criticism (all of which you can interpret as nagging).

Now you can take pride in your own successes and your wife will be proud of you.

MY HUSBAND'S OPINION

My husband, Gerald, went from doing absolutely nothing to making my second full-time job and life a piece of cake.

When I asked him a while back what he thought about all he does around the house, he said, "I don't do anything."

I laughed as I said, "Think back to how it used to be. Remember the old days when you really didn't do anything?"

He was a little surprised. He thought for a minute and then he said, "You know, doing all that I do now is a whole lot easier and more fun than my life was then." He added, "It's so much easier to be involved with everything in the family than to have you mad at me all the time."

He was right. We spent so much time arguing and being mad at each other that it was exhausting. After he started being a responsible partner on the home front, he laughed and joked and became so much more relaxed and fun to be with too.

PICK YOUR OWN CHORES

Stake out some areas in the household that you think you could do all the time. All the typical chores in a household are listed at the back of the book. Go down the list of chores and designate the ones that fit you well enough so they don't seem like such a chore. Negotiate with your wife over any tasks she hates doing that you could tolerate (or enjoy) doing—and earn major gratitude from your sweetie!

COACH YOUR WIFE

I must say this here and repeat it in "Take the Lead in the House-holder Contract" chapter because it is so important. This will be hard advice for your wife. You may have to remind her—patiently—and coach her until she gets used to the change. When you own your list of chores, she must accept the way you do them—no criticism, no nagging. You might not do something exactly the way she does. I encourage her to consider relaxing her standards if she is a neatnik. Or, who knows? She may find that you do things as well or better!

A STORY TO SHARE WITH HER

One of the chores in our Household Contract negotiations that I left totally to my husband was the yard. For years I had taken immense pride in the beauty I'd created. But I realized during our division of tasks that I could relinquish my control to Gerald. If he did it poorly or infrequently, it wouldn't bug me as much as, say, un-vacuumed rugs.

When the yard started looking neglected and the flower bed became a thing of the past, I ignored them completely. They were no longer my responsibility.

Then something spectacular happened. Gerald began taking pride in doing this chore. His manicured yard soon put mine to shame. He was increasingly proud of his project and loved it when people would call on him to ask for advice.

* * *

ALL HOUSEHOLD CHORES UP FOR GRABS

Dennis came in for a haircut. He had heard about my first book and started discussing it, half mockingly.

He said, "I work very hard on my job. Why should I do housework too?"

I teased him back. "Does she work very hard on her job?"

Dennis laughed, "She sits down all day in an office, how hard could that be?"

He added, "I mow the lawn, wash the cars, and do all the outside work. She can do all the stuff inside."

"Hmm," I mused, "How often do you mow the lawn and wash the cars?"

He thought for a minute and didn't answer me.

"For the rest of my life?!"

I pulled out a copy of my book and said, "Why don't you go through the list of chores in the back of the book and choose four or five chores that you could do for the rest of your life."

He whirled his chair around and said, "For the rest of my life?!"

I calmly stated, "Why not? She works just like you do, and when she comes home she has seventy-six more chores that she has to do for the rest of her life."

"I understand now"

He didn't say anything. He took the book and read the chore list while he was still sitting in my salon. They had one toddler and three children in grade school, so all the chores hit home.

"No wonder she's mad at me all the time," he said, sounding rather shell-shocked. "She never told me I was supposed to be responsible for any of that."

I believed him. First his mother and then his wife probably had just asked him to help once in a while. His wife grew angry when he didn't automatically keep helping. Or when he didn't read her mind while she was drowning in a sea of expectations.

Jumping into action

Dennis took the bull by the horns and insisted on taking his turn cooking, buying groceries, watching the baby, and other chores.

Since then, over haircuts, we've have had numerous conversations about how he sometimes has to insist to his wife that she is just as important as he is, and how sorry he is that he hadn't acted on that before.

This is a success story where "sharing" banished the troublesome "help." It's a story that I hope becomes typical as more men are exposed to the chore list.

REMINDERS:

- Stop struggling with "help" and step up to "sharing responsibilities" around the home.

- By shifting your perspective from "help" to sharing householder chores, you will free your wife to have fun with you . . . in the bedroom.

- Select your share of householder chores (on a forever basis, just as your wife will), and do them on your own schedule, in your own way—no nagging allowed! See end of book for chore list.

- Coach you wife patiently until she gets used to the change.

NEED CONVINCING? WALK A WEEK IN HER SHOES

Why dust the house when you can wait another couple of years and get a snow blower?

—Author unknown

Roll your mind back to when you and your wife were childless and you witnessed friends' children in the midst of temper tantrums or their house in chaos. Remember how inept you thought that the parents were, because you, in your childless wisdom, thought you knew exactly how to handle everything? You were sure you'd never allow your child to scream like that, or have a bra end up on the living room floor.

YOUR WIFE WAS CLUELESS

Until your wife was thrust into the chaos of motherhood, she had no idea. Only from on-the-job-training did she learn that the screaming, the vomiting, the clutter, and the toilet training mistakes are part of life. Only then did she learn that the events themselves become the boss. Her job became dealing with the events as they happen, not just preventing them.

YOU COULD DO SO MUCH BETTER

As a husband, you might still be stuck in this phase of childless wisdom if you have never experienced full-time parenting and full-time housekeeping. Not a morning, or a day, but 24/7. Not with a babysitter or your wife, but on your own. From your point of view, you know you could do it so much better. Hey, it's a piece of cake! You can't help but express your bravado. Not yet.

IF YOU "GET IT"

If you "get it" by reading the list of chores (at the back of the book) and then seize ownership of your share of householder tasks—*then you can skip this chapter.*

IF YOU NEED CONVINCING

If you are harder to convince, consider this: It's almost impossible to know what it takes to run a marriage household with children, even if you lived on your own as a bachelor. It's hard to have compassion for another person's problems when you have never experienced them yourself.

Until you participate in everyday household activities and take care of children for more than a weekend at a time, you will remain oblivious—no matter how caring, loving, and wonderful of a husband you are.

FULL IMMERSION THERAPY

I had to resort to a strike. You can take the high road. Send your wife off with her best friend for a week's vacation or to a workshop she's always wanted to attend. The kids stay with you. No babysitters. You are in charge. Your time to shine!

After your full immersion, take the lead in householder contract (see chapter 9).

AVOID REGRETS

I didn't go on strike until our children were all in school. Time flies, and now we have grandchildren. Just recently, my husband was watching three young women with their babies and toddlers, and he marveled at the joy emanating from those little ones. "You know,"

Gerald said, "I never got to experience that in our children, did I?"

"What neither of us realized," I said as I squeezed his hand, "was that while I was allowing you to be gone all the time and not insisting that you help with the kids, I thought I was being a good wife. Instead, I was also robbing you of the wonder and magic that comes with those beginning years, as hard as they sometimes are."

I felt a surge of guilt. The joy I got from our little ones was so beyond explanation that I often think, If I had any part of my life to live over, it would most certainly be that time when our children were little. No matter how hard it was, I would do it again in a heartbeat.

AN UNPLANNED IMMERSION EXAMPLE

Here is a story from one of my clients about the husband who took over all responsibilities for children and home during a medical crisis. The results skyrocketed the love between husband and wife.

Carrie had been my client since she was thirteen. I'd gone through the teen years with her and a disastrous first marriage where physical violence, drugs, and a husband who wouldn't get a job were the realities. Carrie finally divorced and was terrified to get into another relationship.

Afraid to rock the love boat

After a few years, however, she found her soul mate in Don. He was everything her first husband was not, and he would become a wonderful father to their three children. But by the time the children came along, the problem of unbalanced householder work had been rearing its ugly head. Carrie had lived with worse and was reluctant to rock the boat even though Don gave her a hard time about the condition of the house when he came home each night.

Husband gets a week with kids

One day, Carrie got a call from an aunt, saying that her mother was sick and Carrie would have to fly out for a week. Don told her to go. He'd take a week off work and take care of the three little ones.

When his wife returned, Don was in shock from the barrage of daily crises and the mind-numbing mountain of work he'd handled at home.

Marriage soars to new high

"I don't know how you do it all," he told Carrie. "What can I do to make things more fair?" They sat down at the table and split householder chores before going to bed.

Their already wonderful marriage hit a new high.

REMINDERS:

- Even if you lived on your own as a bachelor, it's almost impossible to know what it takes to run a marriage household with children.

- Conduct your own boot camp of full-time parenting and full-time housekeeping. Not a morning or a day, but 24/7 for a week. Not with a babysitter or your wife, but on your own.

- Look at the list of Householder Tasks at the end of the book. Put your name on chores you will do permanently to balance the load that your wife has been carrying by herself.

CHAPTER 9

TAKE THE LEAD IN THE HOUSEHOLDER CONTRACT

Marrying is easy. It's housework that's hard.

—Proverb

I had a client whose wake-up call made me laugh out loud. I asked him to write it in his own words:

My name is Jimmy, and I was a clueless but hardworking (at work) husband. Here's my story. I loved my job. I would go in early and stay late. As usual, when I came home, I sat down to a nice meal with my family cooked by my wife in our spotless kitchen.

Ahhh, to rest after a long day

On this evening, after eating, I leaned back, stretched my hands behind my head, and said, "It will be so nice to go upstairs, get between the sheets, and read."

POW! Her fist connected. She hit me square in the eye with all the force of her pent up anger!

A shiner wake-up call

I wasn't taking any responsibility for our three young kids, meal preparation, grocery shopping, cleanup—or any of the hundred other tasks needed to keep our household running—that she was having to do alone.

At work the next morning, no one would believe my petite, loving wife gave me that shiner. But I knew I deserved her angry punch.

DEEP-DOWN RECOGNITION?

My husband, Gerald, told me that deep down (perhaps in the darkest corner of a coal mine?) some husbands realize their wives are doing so much more for them than they are for their wives, family, and home. And they know too that their wives have been letting them skate past their share.

READERS KNOW THE REALITY

From my decades of research listening to couples, however, I am convinced that the majority of men are clueless about the double burden wives carry and how much they suffer under the weight of doing it all. But whatever the case, because *you* are reading this book, you know the truth.

Maybe your wife is so bitter she's ready to leave you. Maybe her anger is eating at her insides, making her sick, and you're worried about her health. I hope it hasn't gotten that dangerous for you and your family.

BECOME A SUPERHERO

Here's your opportunity to become a superhero. Ride to her rescue in real life, not on screen or in the imagination. Save her from having to "do it all." Become her hero again—like the man who courted her and won her hand.

The Householder (Fair Marriage) Contract and Householder Chore Lists at the back of this book go straight to the heart of fixing and permanently removing the underlying marital bitterness, fighting, and falling out of love that result from your wife having to "do it all."

Householder contract

Read through the Fair Marriage Contract. That gives you a window on what a wife considers fair and reasonable. The framework started with a modified employee-employer union contract—what my husband dealt with all the time in his work.

You are ready and capable

Then turn to Appendix C, the Householder Chore Lists. Some strong men break into a sweat at the sight, but I know you are ready and capable of stepping up to the plate for your share.

Your mission is to put your name beside jobs you will do permanently. That will reduce the workload of your wife . . . relieve her stress, show her respect, give her time to relax, and open up time to spend with you. What an aphrodisiac that would be for her!

TIP FROM A MAN

A reader of my first book shared with me some smart tips for making men's lives better. I asked him to write his key advice in his own words:

My name is John, and I have a tip for you. Perhaps it won't need to be a fifty-fifty split of chores if you choose to do what I call "high-value tasks."

My wife told me that she appreciated my switching loads of laundry and doing a load of dishes, but that those two tasks had low value for her. Her reasoning was that it was easy for her to fit them into her routine.

High-value tasks—big rewards

Contrast that to when I deep-cleaned one of the bathrooms. That turned out to be a high-mileage, high-value activity. Cleaning baseboards and the refrigerator turned out to be high-value tasks as well.

She said she didn't like to do the bathrooms. They took more time and effort, plus she had cleaned a thousand bathrooms over her "career."

When I did a high-value task—the results in our relationship were immediate and enormously satisfying . . . for both of us. If you know what I mean.

Amazing long-term results

We men need to understand that the long-term results will be amazing. You can handle the short-term pain. Just keep doing the right thing.

WHAT ARE HER PREFERENCES?

To determine what chores are "high value" in your wife's mind, put your heads together over the chore list. Also ask her what chores she hates. Those too will give you high mileage if you are willing and able to take charge of them.

I'll chime in with my own preference. A man told me the other day that two of the things he does are to help their older children with their homework and get the little ones to bed every night. I would consider those high-value chores.

Existing chores

As you choose your chores, be sure to put your name on things that you already do. Like yard work, taking care of the cars—whatever you already do. These things will be part of your list. Your wife will learn to appreciate that you've already been contributing and that she won't have to do those chores herself. (She's probably been taking them for granted until now.)

No grades

Also, find some chores that you know you can do your own way. Choose something that won't have to be graded by the-woman-who-lets-you-live-with-her.

Hard advice for your wife

Tell your wife that she may need to relax her standards for work completed by you. When you take on a job, you might not do it the exact way she is used to having it done. You will do your tasks your way—and maybe even better.

MY ADJUSTMENT

One of the things we agreed would go on Gerald's list was the basement. That way, if he didn't get to it as soon as I would have liked, it wouldn't matter because the basement was out of the main traffic area.

Not your mother, teacher, or critic

Let your wife know that you don't want her to tell you how to do your householder work (unless you specifically ask for advice). You can only take on permanent responsibilities if you can be self-directed and take pride in what you accomplish. She is not to be your mother or your teacher or your critic. Tell her to accept your choices.

Ask her which chores she can keep her nose out of—to foster peace!

Deal with failures, successes

You may forget to do a chore. Tell her not to nag about it or do it for you. In the end, you will deal with your own failures and be proud of your own successes.

Warning

Your wife might be one of those wives who are so hardwired culturally to expect to do all the householder work *and* at the same time, grow bitter and angry at their husbands. She still expects to keep the house in perfect shape all by herself, even if she has small children, and even if she has a full-time job. Her whole identity is wrapped up in whether she is a good enough mother and good enough wife. It's easier, she believes, to overwork herself and to continue to be angry all the time—and to resent you and the kids for it.

You can either accept the resentment and the anger, or you can coach her and try to create the change yourself. Make it easier for both of you.

> NOTE: If you get serious blowback from your willingness to take charge of your share of the householder tasks, read Appendix A. Have your wife read it too. It's my "the gloves are off" message to wives who are angry but won't give up control.

Consider a domestic service

If both of you have hectic, more-than-full-time work schedules, think seriously about hiring a domestic service. Hiring someone to do a half-dozen or so weekly time-consuming cleaning tasks will give both of you more freedom to be with your children at school functions and sports. And freedom from guilt as you waltz across the kitchen floor—into each other's arms.

ROLE MODEL FOR YOUR KIDS

By doing your share of household chores, you will set a good example for your children—now and in their own adult relationships. Your sons and daughters will have the knowledge and experience to automatically start off on the right foot in their relationships.

PICK HER UP OFF THE FLOOR

By proposing to split the householder chores, you probably will put your wife in a delirious state of shock—one that will earn you a lifetime of respect and love. Pick her up off the floor and assure her that this is no dream!

REMINDERS:

- Become a superhero. Fix and remove the underlying marital bitterness, fighting, and falling out of love that result from your wife having to "do it all" in your household.

- Your mission is to put your name beside jobs you will do permanently (listed at the back of the book in the Householder Tasks section of the Fair Marriage Contract.

- Showing your wife this respect and giving her time to relax will be a major aphrodisiac.

CHAPTER 10
WHAT'S IN IT FOR ME?

The secret to a happy marriage isn't finding the right person;
it is being the right person.

Here's the bottom line. From a man:

THE VALUE OF A HAPPY WIFE

The value of a happy wife is hard to describe adequately. Every man knows that awesome feeling when your wife is happy, you two are in sync with each other, all cylinders firing. Men can't describe it very well, but every man who has experienced it will tell you there is nothing better in the world. It's like the feeling during courtship—but better, because your relationship has matured.

Worth walking over hot coals!

If men could really see the rewards of sharing the householder work-load and understand how their lives would be enriched, men would walk over hot coals to get there.

I couldn't say it better!

Society's wall

Society and our upbringing—yours and hers—combine to build a wall that blocks this happiness. The chapters in this book give you knowledge and tools to demolish that wall and rebuild your loving relationship.

WHICH DOOR WOULD YOU CHOOSE?

What's in it for you? Well, would you rather be sending part of your salary to your divorce lawyer? Or be embraced by your lovely wife (and children) for years to come?

I've had men—and women—stop me to say, "Thank you. Your book has saved my marriage. And my family."

RESEARCH FINDINGS

Psychologist Joshua Coleman, who gave me permission to quote him in this book, found the following to be true:

- Men who regularly do housework are associated with wives who are more interested in sex.
- Women with partners who are actively involved in parenting and housework are happier and more satisfied with their marriage.
- Women who do the majority of housework and childcare in a family are more prone to physical illness and more likely to become depressed.
- Women are far more likely to think about divorce when they are married to men who neglect the house and kids.
- School-age children who do housework with the fathers have more friends at school and are more likely to get along well with others. They are also less likely to disobey teachers.
- Children score higher on academic tests in homes where dad is more involved.[1]

MALE READER'S STORY

The following story illustrates how sharing householder tasks can reward you.

I gave Nathan, a client, a copy of my first book, urging him to read it and report back to me. Sharon, his wife and also my client, earlier had complained to me that every time Nathan helped her, he would expect to be thanked. If Sharon didn't thank him, he thought he should stop helping.

What did you think?

A lot of time passed, and I began to doubt that I'd hear from him. Then he made an appointment. The anticipation was killing me!

When he came in, he had the book and told me I hadn't signed it. I tried to hold my tongue for at least a minute. It didn't work.

I blurted out, "Well—what did you think?"

"Ever since you chastised me for not pitching in at home," he said with a chuckle, "I have been trying to help Sharon with the house and kids."

Expecting thanks for helping

"Sharon was right, however," he said. "When I did things to help her, I expected to be thanked. I expected to be thanked in more ways than one. If you know what I mean."

I knew what he meant. That all-too-familiar fallacy . . . if I do this for her, she will automatically want to jump in the sack with me."

"Sherri is full of crap"

"It didn't happen." He said. "I thought once or twice through the whole process, 'Sherri is full of crap.' "

We both laughed.

"After I read your book," he said, "I could see why she was still upset."

Chores that are mine alone

"We both went to the back of the book and designated specific chores that were mine and mine alone.

"Of course, it was a little difficult at first," he said. "It was definitely something I wasn't used to."

Bragging on kids

"Part of my job is helping the older kids with their homework and getting the little ones to bed." He said. "As time consuming as that is, I actually enjoy interacting with my kids."

Then I heard words used by every proud parent: "You wouldn't believe how smart Dillon is!"

In all the time I had known Nathan, I had never heard him brag about his kids. Come to think of it: I had never heard him mention his kids. Now that he was involved with so much of their lives, he was obviously beginning to sense that as hard as it is to take care of a rambunctious brood, the rewards far outweigh the hardships to a phenomenal degree.

Nathan went on and on, telling me some of the funny things the children said and did.

New respect for wife

He said, "You know, when I looked at your householder chore list, I realized that Sharon has done a lot more than I had ever given her credit for. It made me appreciate and love her so much more."

He seemed like a whole new person. He seemed so much more content. He seemed so much more relaxed.

Fantastic sex life

I brazenly asked, "How's your sex life?"

After he almost fell on the floor at my bluntness, he asked, "How did you know?" Then he added, "Have you been talking to Sharon?"

"I'm asking you." I said with a grin.

"It's fantastic," he said.

She even intiates sex

He was a little embarrassed. He needn't have been. He was talking to an old lady who had heard it all.

"Do you know," he said, "for the first time in our married life, she has actually initiated sex a few times."

It had only been a couple of months since he made changes, so I knew that number would climb by hundreds.

Remove obstacles

Then he added, "When I was just helping her with what I considered her responsibilities and expecting something in return, it was a nightmare. I can see why now."

Lack of sex can be alleviated much of the time by removing obstacles preventing that intimacy. Exhaustion, resentment, and anger are just a few of those obstacles.

WANTING TIME ON HER LIST

I had interviewed a man who was extremely upset about the lack of intimacy in his marriage.

He told me, "My wife has a journal she keeps every day. One day I noticed her journal on the counter and began to read it. I noticed that the journal was completely full of endless tasks, sometimes three pages for one day."

What would you say?

I have told this story numerous times. At this point I asked the listeners what they think he said next.

The unanimous answer was always, "He wondered what he could do to help her."

What he really said

What he really said was, "Where am I on that list?"

That sounds a bit selfish, doesn't it? Now I know you men are thinking I am picking on you, but I'm not. The fact is, I laughed at what the man said, and I gave him a pass.

Cumulative damage

The tasks in his wife's daily journal individually may take only five minutes or so each. It didn't dawn on the husband, however, that all together the tasks are so cumulatively time-consuming and exhausting that she wouldn't have the energy or the time to think of pleasuring him. I can actually picture her having a headache when it's time for sex!

My answer to this man on how he could get on her list: "Why don't you go down the list and find two or three things you can take off of her list, something you can do yourself. Then you can put your name there."

NO DIME TIP!

Always remember that if you do a task today just so you can get sex that night, forget it. That's like going to a fancy restaurant, having fantastic service, and leaving the waitress a dime for her tip. It's not about work. It's about respect and long-term cooperation.

KISSES FOR THE FUN OF KISSING

What you need to do on a regular basis is go up and put your arms around her for no reason, maybe even give her a kiss and DO NOT EXPECT IT TO LEAD ANYWHERE. If you do that on a regular basis, your sex life will improve dramatically, especially if you already are a participating partner on the home front.

REPLACE RESENTMENT WITH SEX

Dr. John Gottman, marital researcher, has found that when a man does his share of housework, both he and his wife report a more satisfying sex life than in marriages where the wife believes the husband isn't doing his share.[2]

Remember, resentment never leads to intimacy. The fact is that resentment leads to no intimacy.

ARGUE LESS, LOVE MORE

When my husband began doing his share of household tasks, our sex life hit a whole new level. Our arguments were 80 percent fewer than when I was doing it all. Fewer arguments are a reward in themselves.

REMINDERS:

- If men could realize the rewards of sharing household work and understand how their lives would be enriched, they would walk over hot coals to get there.

- If you do a task today only so you can get sex tonight—forget it! That's like eating at a fancy restaurant and leaving a dime tip.

- It's all about respect and long-term cooperation for your wife.

- Kiss for the tenderness of kissing, hug for loving only, but don't expect either to lead anywhere. Surprisingly, doing that daily will improve your sex life far beyond your expectations.

NOTES

1. Joshua Coleman, *The Lazy Husband: How to Get Men to Do More Parenting and Housework* (New York: St. Martin's Press, 2005).

2. John Gottman, *Why Marriages Succeed or Fail.*

MEN OF FAITH

Whatever you are, be a good one.

—Abraham Lincoln

Maybe you are a man in a very strict religion, where one of the rules is that the man is the head of the house and no one is to question his authority. The fact that your wife is submissive, however, doesn't eliminate problems.

BENEFITS FROM THIS BOOK

I'm not saying that any religion is wrong in how it handles household situations. What I am saying is that a husband of faith will benefit from what I suggest in this book as much as other husbands.

NEVER PERFECT

Your wife, in her effort to remain respectful to you, may not be as vocal about her overwhelming workload. This does not mean that it doesn't exist. You may experience silent sadness, depression, or other maladies in your wife. They come from a woman who is overworked, underappreciated, and unsure about how to speak up.

NOT ON PURPOSE

These maladies just happen—they're not purposely planned by your wife to make your life miserable, nor are you to blame for their occurrence.

There are even explosions in religious families. They just manifest themselves in different ways. As a consequence, however, you have to work overtime to learn what's bothering your wife and how you might fix it.

NO DEMANDS, NO DISRESPECT

Nowhere in my writing do I advocate wives making demands, disrespecting a husband, or exerting one's power to get results. All of these methods have been demonized by me in my books. These flawed methods are part of the reason why I didn't get results in the first twelve years of my own marriage.

Instead, I suggest that women do whatever it takes to make certain their situation is understood. I stress that this is not accomplished with screams, shouts, or demands. It is only accomplished with peace, love, understanding, and, most important, all the fortitude a woman can muster.

GOAL—SOCIETY SUPPORTS SHARING

My ultimate goal is that soon responsibility for domesticity will not be seen as solely a woman's issue, or as emasculating to men—that men and women will naturally consider household tasks a joint venture. All the deciding and dividing will be done before the marriage, and all of our society will admit that householder work (including raising children) should be shared.

HEAD OF HOUSEHOLD BELIEFS

My very religious cousin sat in my living room, talking about my book. He held "man is the head of the house" beliefs.

He said, "I know how much Susan does. She is exhausted all the time."

I said, "What do you think about that?"

He said, "Well I really do appreciate everything she does."

Are thanks enough?

"So what do you do about it?" I asked.

"I tell her thank you all the time."

"Hmm. Do you really think that is enough?"

I didn't wait for an answer. I said, "I can't even imagine how she does it all with your eight kids." I began naming all the things that have to be done daily in a household that size.

He stopped me when I reached the twentieth chore.

Antidepressants

He said, "I never looked at it like that." Then he said, "No wonder she needs antidepressants."

Being the outspoken person that I am, I said, "She will be on anti-depressants until you shape up and take as much responsibility with the house and children as she does."

You see, I wasn't the wife who was supposed to put him on a pedestal. I was his ever-belligerent, bigmouth cousin who could say anything I wanted, and he took it.

You are a householder too

I continued, only kinder now. "What you might do," I said, "is insist that she let you do your share. Look in the back of my book and pick out a number of chores you can tell her you will do from now on."

I let him know that his wife was hardwired to make him happy and do everything for him (despite being silently resentful and sad because she was overwhelmed knowing she couldn't do it all). He would have to take the bull by the horns by picking out some chores from the back of the book and insisting that they be his responsibilities from now on. To tell her that what makes him happy is to see her happy.

I told him to be sure and pick chores where he and his wife would be comfortable if he did them his way.

New perspective

I spoke with him recently. He thanked me for being so blunt. He said, "I had no idea."

No one ever does until they do it for themselves.

REMINDERS:

- Even in strictly religious families, great relationships aren't guaranteed. You may be facing her depression, resentment, constant nagging, or silent sadness.

- Don't just thank her for all she does. Become engaged with your share of householder tasks. You will be surprised how much easier it is to be involved than to worry and wonder what is wrong.

- The ultimate goal: soon responsibility for domesticity won't even be an issue. All the deciding and dividing will be done before the marriage, and all of our society will admit that householder work (including raising children) should be shared.

CHAPTER 12

TIP FROM FORREST GUMP: "LISTEN"

"I'm not a smart man. But I know what love is."

—Forrest Gump

I've heard men say, "Forrest Gump wasn't the smartest guy, but he was brilliant at listening."

Listening can be such a wonderful tool for making it easier for your wife to let you know how she feels about the double duty and double standard of householder work. This is an area where she would like you to listen and then act.

Not all listening requires action, however. It's important that you work to build a relationship where your wife feels comfortable coming to you just to talk about anything. That way, she'll feel relaxed and understood and be less likely to build up a month's, a year's, or a lifetime's worth of resentment.

BE THERE FOR HER

A fan of that Tom Hanks movie said to me, "Forrest Gump never tried to solve Jennie's issues. Most of the time, he just sat there and listened. Didn't say a word. Maybe put his arm around her.

"If he did talk, it was short sentences like 'I'm sorry,' or 'I like you, Jennie.' Just supporting her."

He told me, "Watch that movie and just focus on his ability to listen and be there for someone."

WONDER DRUG OF MARRIAGES

Communication is the medicine that can cure rocky stretches in a relationship. It is also the glue that will bond you and your wife tightly together. Heck, it's really the wonder drug of marriages.

The ability to listen is probably its most valuable component.

CALM YOUR TENDENCY TOWARD ACTION

When told something is wrong, men automatically prefer action. You want to jump in and fix things. Sometimes in marriage, listening—not solving—is what your wife really needs.

BAD MEETING / BAD DAY

Patricia slammed the front door as she came home from her meeting and threw her coat and briefcase down on a chair. "Oh, those Neanderthals. How could they still be spouting the same old, same old!

Her husband, Jake, came in from the other room, took her hand, and led her to the couch.

"Tell me what happened," he said.

Women need to complain

For the next ten minutes, Patricia talked, her voice alternately rising and falling in anger and sadness.

Finally she sighed, snuggled against Jake, and kissed him. "Thanks, honey, I needed that. I feel better now. And I think I know what my next approach will be."

Soothe, not solve

Jake didn't jump in to fix his wife's problem by telling her his own solution. That was unnecessary and would have been counterproductive. What she really needed now was a sounding board for her complaints. He filled her need by *soothing* her frustration over the problem with respectful listening.

He knew that she would find her own way. If she really did want his advice, she would ask directly for it—maybe tomorrow when she could be analytical about her crisis.

Even Forrest Gump knew that

In the emotional aftermath of a bad meeting (or a bad day), a woman just wants to complain to a sympathetic ear. She wants her husband to understand and appreciate that she had a bad day, not try to fix it. Weird, but that's what women want. Even Forrest Gump knew that.

Talk out loud

In addition to listening, men also need to learn how to do the opposite: talk! John, a counselor who was one of my psychology advisers, told me, "Men can improve their relationships simply by learning to talk out loud."

He said, and I agree, "Women want to know what we are thinking."

He said, "Men have a habit of expecting women to read their minds, not intentionally of course. However, very often in my practice when I have a couple in my office, the woman says 'he expects me to know exactly what he is thinking without ever telling me'."

"Practice talking and thinking out loud like women do," he suggests. "Even if you do it a little bit, that would make a big difference."

It may not come naturally at first, but in the end, you'll find that your communication as a couple will be strengthened, resulting in both of your needs better being met.

Face-to-face time

John offered another observation and tip: Women build rapport face to face, while men build rapport side by side.

Think about it. Men will go fishing and stand side-by-side all day and just love it. Women will turn their chairs to face each other and look at each other while they talk.

Use your smartphone for reminders

John suggested that men put a reminder on their smartphones to spend fifteen minutes "today" face-to-face with their wives. Both listening and talking.

He added, "Eventually men will see the results, and face-to-face time will become automatic, a normal part of their day." He advised, "You really have to do it daily because this is a need your wife has that a man probably doesn't."

All of these tips on listening can make it so much easier for your wife to explain what she is hiding, or hurting from, like how unequal household responsibilities are. She will need to know for sure that you hear her so she can get her point across without releasing her anger.

WATCH THE "MY" LANGUAGE

One of the mistakes I made for years was to refer to the children as "my kids," the house as "my house," and the kitchen as "my kitchen." How could I expect my husband to take ownership when my language made it clear that these parts of the house, and even the children, were mine and not ours?

I've learned!

I verbally excluded my husband from those parts of our life, and then I resented him for not taking on any of their inherent responsibilities. Dumb. But I've learned!

You may need to gently coach your wife when you hear her use "my" instead of "our" for parts of the house or for your children. Watch how you use that word too. It's all about sharing and practicing the right language.

NEEDING TO BE RIGHT VERSUS BEING HAPPY

Listen up! The following tips are worth their weight in gold for your marriage.

Do you need to win every argument? Or have the last word? Do your discussions turn into arguments because someone has to be right?

When you need to be right all the time, you create a special place in your brain to store all of your partner's wrongdoings. That way, in the midst of an argument, you can go to your memory bank, pluck out a wrongdoing, and win. Even if that wrong doing happened weeks, months, or years ago. You keep doing this even though "being right" ultimately jeopardizes "being happy" in your relationship.

How You React

Remember why you loved your wife in the early days, the days when you were deeply in love? Remember when you first met what it was that made her stand out from other women? Remember the personality traits you loved about her?

Is it possible that after you married, your interactions with each other are what make everything difficult? Is it possible that it isn't your partner's actions but *how you react* to them that creates the problem?

In such a relationship, the memories of ugly arguments and disappointments shout louder and crowd out happy, loving, delightful memories and put you on guard, ready to fight first and listen later.

Go for the Higher Level

Needing to be right muddles your brain. You will be happier if you can reach that higher level in your relationship where being right isn't all that important. Then you can toss out the negative garbage in your brain to clear a neural pathway to your real treasures—the loving memories—so they are near the surface and the first to be remembered.

Remember that you are in charge of your own thoughts. When your thoughts get stuck on what's wrong instead of what's right, you have little room for the best kind of thinking—positive thinking.

Make sure that being right doesn't get in the way of getting results.

Bickering & Fighting

Reflect on how tiring it is for you to always have to be right and how that halts progress. If you both have to be right, then the bickering and the fighting will be never ending. Yes, you can both feel powerful and beat your chest in victory over your spouse, but is that what marriage is about? Have you solved anything by dealing with your problems in that way?

Your wife is the person whose friendship and love you wanted for the rest of your life. And she can still be that person, unless you have to be right.

Train your brain to replace this negative form of talking with loving thoughts and strategies.

REMINDERS:

- Communication can bridge rocky stretches in a relationship. Call it the glue that bonds you and your wife together.

- Listen to her problems—don't try to fix them—unless she specifically asks for advice. Often she just needs to vent.

- Needing to be right all the time—win every argument—defeats a good relationship.

CHAPTER 13

TALK! EVEN IF IT HURTS

Don't wait. The time may never be just right.

—Napoleon Hill

To paraphrase the husband in the movie *P.S. I Love You*: "Okay! I did it! I did it! I'm really sorry. Truly I am. Honey, just tell me what I did."

I can't stress enough that just because your wife says nothing when you see her upset, doesn't mean everything is hunky-dory. Don't fall into the trap and give up.

IT'S NEVER NOTHING

Ask your wife what is wrong. If she says, "Nothing," don't let it go. It is never nothing. No matter how long it takes, make peace with the issue.

Tell her gently and honestly that you will do whatever you can do to make it better. Let her know that you may not be able to do exactly what she wants, so it is important to ask her what she can live with, and then figure out some kind of a compromise.

THE POWER OF A WISE COUNSELOR

One thing I have discovered is that communication is automatic when you're in therapy. Sometimes it's not very comfortable because negative feelings are bubbling out from both parties. However, all of this is happening in a safe environment and under professional guidance. There's no bolting from the therapist's office because one person doesn't like what he or she hears. Therapy forces hurts out into the open so they can be examined and resolved by both parties.

Talk! Even if it hurts

It's a crazy-making situation when you go through days—or years, as in the following marriage story—being punished when you have no idea what you did wrong.

Here's a case where a couple's love and adoration gradually turned to hate on one side and emotional absence on the other. Three children were watching.

LOVING HUSBAND AND BREADWINNER

My client Bill married Renee, also my client. They had three children and seemed to have a happy life. They both devoted a lot of time to their kids. But then I began to notice something different about Renee. When I questioned her, she said she was suffering from a deep depression.

She was extremely sick for a long time. Bill was wonderful about taking care of her and the kids.

One day, Bill told Renee that he was being transferred to Pennsylvania. The move was a substantial promotion with a lot more money. He couldn't turn it down.

Silent panic

Renee was horrified. Instead of telling Bill of her fears about the move, she came to me with her complaints. Her family all lived in Utah, and she was afraid of losing them. And she was still suffering from chronic depression.

But she put on a happy face, had a yard sale, and packed up everything. Then she moved out East.

With Bill making really good money, she was able to come back for visits. Every time she came home, she would make an appointment with me to get her hair done. When she called, I would mark off a lot of time so we could talk. She had plenty to say. She hated living far away in Pennsylvania.

Bombshell

"Have you talked to Bill about this?" I would ask, hoping to prod her.

"No," she would always reply.

One day she came back to Utah and announced she was planning to stay.

I opened up extra time for her by rearranging a few appointments so we could talk as long as needed.

"Okay," I said, "what's the problem?"

"I hate it there!" she said through a flood of tears.

"It's always hard when you first get to a new place." I said, trying to comfort her.

Wanting an easy way out

"I hate Bill," she cried. "I have filed for divorce. I'm staying here. I'm moving in with my mom."

I knew instinctively that I had my work cut out for me. She was determined.

"Tell me what you hate about him." I asked cautiously, knowing these next words would count.

"We never talk anymore."

"We never talk anymore." She said, still sobbing. "We just pass each other, in the house, like the other one doesn't exist."

"How long has this been going on?" I asked.

"For a long time," she said. "He just comes home, grabs a beer and a paper, sits down, and ignores me and the kids."

Still a mystery to me

I knew Bill didn't ignore the kids because he was always taking them everywhere. And he faithfully took care of her and the kids while she was sick and he was still working. Why she was upset was still a mystery to me.

I had to convince her that divorce would be a miserable mistake before we could even discuss how to make their marriage better.

What will happen after?

"Have you thought about everything that is going to happen after the divorce?" I asked, getting a little bolder.

"Of course I have!" She was adamant "I just don't love Bill anymore."

That's when I started to get testy, showing my negative attitude about divorce.

Face reality

"Well, girl," I said, "You obviously don't know the first thing about what you are in for if you divorce." Without giving her a chance to respond, I continued, "Do you realize how far away Pennsylvania is?"

Again I didn't wait for an answer because I was on a roll. "One thing I know about you is that you worship your children. You would lie down and die for them." She wasn't looking at me, and I think she was just waiting for me to finish.

She wanted my help. However, the help she wanted wasn't to save her marriage. She obviously wanted me to condone her divorce and help her through it.

Good dad

I would have none of it. "So you love your kids so much that you are going to force them to fly to Pennsylvania and back? Of course you know Bill is never going to allow you to keep the kids away from him. And he shouldn't. He's a good dad."

I wasn't finished, but she was sobbing so violently that I decided I had better let up a little.

Old hurts—never resolved

"What can I do? I don't love him." She said between sobs.

"You loved him once," I said, and then very lovingly stated, "You adored him once, so let's figure out what went wrong."

"Well I have never forgiven him for being gone when I had my last baby." She was sobbing. "I almost died, and he didn't come home from his elk hunt to be with me." She continued, "Every time I think about it, I just hate him."

Did he realize?

I thought back at how long ago that must have been. Her baby was now eight years old.

"That was awful." I said. "But is it possible that a man wouldn't realize how completely devastating that would have been?"

Toxic thoughts

I tend to talk fast, but at this moment I was slow and methodical. "Do you realize," I said, "that you have been feeding your body toxic thoughts for eight long years?"

She looked surprised. I asked, "Did you ever tell him how angry you were?"

Did you tell him?

Her negative answer didn't surprise me. Thirty years of listening had taught me that women are masters at hiding their real thoughts from their husbands.

My mind flashed back at how long she had suffered from depression. I said, "The hate and resentment about Bill not being there for your last and difficult birth has been poisoning your body for all that time. And if you think about it, Bill probably never did deserve that blame."

Not guilty

"Before you leave here today, you are going to begin to forgive Bill." I said. I finally had a place to start. "In the first place, knowing Bill, I am sure he came home as soon as he could. If he had known how serious the birth would be, he would have been there for you."

Neither one of us spoke for what seemed to be an eternity.

He didn't know

Then she said, "You know, come to think of it, I didn't really tell him how serious the birth was."

I put my hands on her knees, looked into her face, and said. "See, he didn't know."

All of a sudden, her tears seemed to dry up, and she said, "You know, I think you're right. How could he have known?"

Eight years—eight long years of suffering (on both sides) because nothing was said.

Resolution

Renee went back to her husband in Pennsylvania. Bill was shocked when he discovered why Renee had behaved so hatefully toward him. They are like lovebirds again. I don't know who is happier that she broke her silence—Renee, Bill, or their three kids.

LEARNING RELATIONSHIP SKILLS

I have spoken with many couples that have had ups and downs and long periods of time when they didn't even like each other. But once they learned to skillfully work through their problems, for the sake of their children and for their own sakes, they ended up with happy marriages again. Moreover, their lives were far better than those of their divorced friends. They had a sense of security in one another, solid finances, and could easily grow into being grandparents.

REMINDERS:

- Resolve hurts when they happen—before they magnify.

- When your wife seems very upset and she tells you it's nothing—don't let it go. Get to the bottom of it.

- If you can't communicate, go to a marriage counselor. If you can't afford therapy, there is no way you can afford a divorce.

CHAPTER 14

WHAT MEN DON'T INSTINCTIVELY KNOW

*Don't let what you can't do
stop you from what you can do.*

—John Wooden

I quoted the wisdom of counselor and author Dr. Joshua Coleman earlier in this book. Here is straight talk from him about your life when babies arrive.

One of the biggest sources of male marital satisfaction is sexual frequency.

Unfortunately, during the first year after a child is born, sexual frequency drops in 30 to 40 percent of couples because the wife loses interest due to stress, exhaustion, and hormonal changes. . . .

This causes men to pull back from their wives, feeling rejected or angry.

Tragically, this occurs at a time when their wives need them the most.

Couples appear to make better transition through the trials of a new baby when the husband is able to prioritize his wife's increased need for emotional support and physical involvement, and where she is able to balance her love affair with the baby with her husband's needs for attention, affection, and acknowledgment.[1]

AVOID BEING A STATISTIC

I suggest you can avoid being a statistic where your sexual frequency drops radically. The earlier chapters in this book have given you the tools.

First, understand the mountain of work that comes with having a newborn. No, realize your wife faces a whole *mountain range* of work if other young children are already part of your family.

Second, insist on taking her workload temporarily. And share the sleepless nights, the constant crying, the colic, the interruptions from regular activities, the responsibility that the helpless baby always comes first.

If she has postpartum depression (addressed later in this chapter), let her know you understand and wait it out.

Satisfying equation

Your thoughtfulness will be rewarded. (1) You, like her, will probably be too tired to worry about sex for more than a minute. (2) You will share in the exhilarating pride that comes from miracles of new life that carry your genes. The ultimate joy you will experience will far exceed any amount of work you put in. (3) By shouldering the household workload, you will give her a break and reduce her exhaustion. (4) Your thoughtfulness will avoid a buildup of her resentment because she won't have to "do it all."

(5) These points add up to a satisfying equation: Less exhaustion + more love because of your thoughtfulness + less need for resentment = MORE SEX.

Postpartum depression (PPD)

It's a red flag for action if your wife comes home with a new baby and doesn't seem happy. Not just tired, but sad.

She needs your encouragement to see her doctor about postpartum depression. Accompany her so you can learn more. She also needs for you to refrain from judging her. Let her know you understand and wait for this monster to leave. It will.

Depression and guilt

I'm amazed today that postpartum depression is not more commonly known or discussed—especially by doctors. It's a glitch in the usual hormone changes that sometimes happens when women give birth. The depression—and guilty thoughts—will end when her hormones return to normal. But until then, her life and yours could be miserable.

The following experience illustrates the pain involved when you have no idea what's going on. If it happens to you and your wife, go online and do some research. You will both be glad you did.

My own nightmare

I remember sitting in the rocking chair, holding our beautiful baby boy, who only days earlier had made my world a wonderland. I was the happiest woman on the planet. It seemed I had been waiting years for the moment I would have my first child. My husband and I were both sitting on a cloud. Now I was engulfed by astronomical sadness, a sadness I had no explanation for.

My wonderland had turned into a nightmare of guilty thoughts. I was enveloped by a cloud of gloom so dark and so thick that I couldn't see an escape. All the time, people around me said, "You should be the happiest woman on earth."

I knew I should be happy

Did all these people think I didn't know that? Of course I knew I should be happy! The guilt I felt was almost as heavy as the dark cloud that engulfed my very soul.

My thoughts were completely involuntary. Any amount of my wanting to change them did not make them go away.

They did go away in a few weeks, however, at the time I had no idea what was happening to me. Since that time, I have researched this malady and am dumbfounded at how many mothers have no idea what it is. And if young mothers don't know what to expect, how can we expect fathers to be aware of it, and be prepared?

EDUCATE YOURSELF

Just simply being aware of what might happen after your wife gives birth could give you the preparedness you will need to wait it out with her with love and understanding.

The Department of Health and Human Services gives the following information on PPD:

About 13 percent of new mothers suffer from this malady.

If your wife has any of the following symptoms for more than two weeks, call a doctor:

- Feeling restless or moody
- Feeling sad, hopeless, and overwhelmed
- Crying a lot
- Having no energy or motivation
- Having trouble focusing or making decisions
- Having memory problems
- Feeling worthless or guilty

Hormonal changes may trigger symptoms of PPD. When a woman is pregnant, levels of the hormones estrogen and progesterone increase greatly. In the first twenty-four hours after childbirth, hormone levels quickly return to normal. Researchers think the big change in hormone levels may lead to postpartum depression.[2]

NEEDING UNDERSTANDING AND PATIENCE

Men, understanding on your part during this difficult time is important to the rest of your marriage. Withhold judgment and be patient and supportive. You may have to work harder than ever before to help your wife through this time of depression, anxiety, and fatigue, but I promise that your love life will eventually return, and it will be even better if you have shown her the kind of love and understanding that she needs during this period.

REMINDERS:

- Tackle the mountain of work that comes with a newborn. That will give your wife more energy and time for you.

- When you carry her workload, you may be too exhausted and involved to dwell on how much sex is missing in your life at the moment.

- Encourage your wife to get medical help if she comes home from the hospital with a newborn and is sad instead of happy. Postpartum depression needs your understanding—and her hormones to rebalance.

NOTES

1. Joshua Coleman, *The Lazy Husband: How to Get Men to Do More Parenting and Housework* (New York: St. Martin's Press, 2005).

2. U.S. Department of Health and Human Services, Office on Women's Health, "Depression during and after Pregnancy Fact Sheet," March 6, 2009, http://www.womenshealth.gov/publications/our-publications/fact-sheet/depression-pregnancy.pdf.

CHAPTER 15

Costs: Part One
DIVORCE RARELY EQUALS HAPPINESS

We must become the change we want to see.

—Mahatma Gandhi

I said this in my first book, and it's important to repeat it here:
If happiness were the standard for judging a marriage, divorce would be justified in most marriages once a day.

HAPPINESS VERSUS DIVORCE

A report issued by the Institute for American Values suggests that

1. unhappily married adults who divorced were no happier five years later.

2. Two thirds of unhappily married people who remained married reported that their marriages were happy five years later.[1]

PATIENCE

We just have to make it through the rough spots.

WANTS FAMILY BACK

The other day, I spoke to a man who had been divorced for three years. At the time of his divorce, he was ecstatic to be out. I remember him telling me he was bored to tears in his marriage.

Now he looked embarrassed. We both realized if he hadn't had so much time on his hands from doing nothing on the home front, he wouldn't have been so bored. He wouldn't have chosen to spend his extra time going out. He wouldn't have been looking for an affair.

Her workload left no time for him

He said, "You know Sherri, you're right. My wife was so busy working, running the kids around, cooking, and cleaning, she didn't have any spare time for me."

After his divorce, he had all the freedom to date and party. However, after a few relationships and a marriage that he is still in, he came to me in tears.

Dark side of the fence

He told me that life on the other side of the fence wasn't what it was cracked up to be.

He said, "I was so much happier in my first marriage. I'm still deliriously in love with my ex-wife."

Too late

He hit his fist against the wall and wailed, "I want my wife and kids back. I know it was my fault, but I would do anything to get them back."

It was too late.

THREE MYTHS PUSH DIVORCE AND CLOUD REALITY

There are three major falsehoods that couples in workable relationships use to justify divorce:

(MYTH #1) If you're not happy in your marriage, it's not healthy for you to stay married, nor is it healthy for your children.

(MYTH #2) It's better for children to see their parents divorced than it is to see them together and fighting.

(MYTH #3) It's unhealthy for parents to stay together for the sake of the children.

QUAGMIRE AHEAD!

What's a man to think when you hear such psychobabble? These myths will make a quick-fix divorce seem the answer. But you have no idea the quagmire you are getting yourself and your children into for life.

FOREVER CONNECTED BY THE KIDS

When you have children and you get divorced, you will be connected to your ex-wife for the rest of your life, most of the time you will hate each other. If you can't afford a marriage counselor while you are married, no way will you be able to afford a divorce.

MYTH #1

Let's examine myth #1:

If you're not happy in your marriage, it's not healthy for you to stay married, nor is it healthy for your children.

Life-altering choice—for you and your kids

Happiness is a human emotion, and the lack of it is not the reason to make a life-altering choice. The fact is, if you've ever been happy together, you can get happy again. Your children should not have to become unhappy in the future because you are unhappy now.

Loved once, loved now

Remember, you loved your wife when you courted and married her. Now you have children you adore. On paper that sounds better than happy. That sounds ecstatic. But we all know that life is not a fairy tale. Along with those angelic children come mountains of work and hardships.

Kids worth the hardships

To cope with the work and hardships, you seek a solution. You think that even though your children require you to work and sacrifice, you would never kick them out because they are worth all the trouble. So you think if you get rid of your nagging, angry, dowdy wife you will be happier?

What if?

What if the reason she is nagging is because she is overwhelmed doing everything by herself?

What if the reason she is angry is because she has to work all day at work and then come home to another full-time job?

What if the reason she is dowdy is because she has absolutely no free time or energy to fix herself up and make herself sexy for you?

What if she is still the same wonderful gal you fell in love with, but she needs your cooperation so both of you can enjoy your marriage together.

You can get happy again

If you are unhappy in your marriage, you can get happy again. The key is in discovering specifically what you want and then using a successful program to get it.

Talk with a marriage counselor

Going to a marriage counselor is a great way to start. If you can't get your wife to go to a counselor, go by yourself. She may follow. If she doesn't, you will still add new life skills to your toolbox, and you'll be able to use these in the relationship to fix or avoid traps you would have fallen into in the past.

Nothing beats family and children

You will find that no hardship is big enough to even come close to matching the colossal joy that comes from family and children.

MYTH #2

Now let's examine myth #2:

It's better for children to see their parents divorced than to see them fighting all the time.

RIDICULOUS!

How ridiculous is that? Really! If you are fighting all the time while you're married, you will continue to fight after the divorce.

Fighting over the children

It's a lot harder to get along when you are going through a divorce than when you are married. And you will be going through the divorce for the rest of the children's lives. Only now when you fight, you'll be fighting over the children. They will know that.

Children believe divorce is their fault

Children will think more and more that all the fighting is their fault. Will the children later see divorce as the answer to any fight and want to leave YOU as they struggle through the teenage years?

No such thing as a good divorce

According to clinical psychologist Dr. Liz Hale, there may not be such a thing as a good divorce.

"Sure, we will all move on," she writes in an article, "but to what degree does the sting of divorce remain for all involved? Divorce requires children to exist somewhere between two homes.

Children carry scars into adulthood

Dr. Hale observed, "Whenever I speak to adult children of divorce, certain key phrases are repeated: My loyalties were always split; I never know where I fit in; I was always saying good-bye to one of my parents; or I had to be a little adult dealing with grown-up issues."

LESSONS LEARNED BY CHILDREN

Children who come from divorced families have a higher likelihood of divorcing. Perhaps divorce teaches children that problems can't be solved.

One afternoon, John came into the salon after a huge battle with his wife and stated that he was quitting his job and moving to Denver.

"What's in Denver?" I asked.

"Nothing," he said, "I just thought Denver would be a good place for a new start."

"Aren't you going to try and work on your marriage?" I asked as I doused him with the spray bottle.

"I'd just as soon find somebody else."

"She drives me nuts," he said "I'd just as soon find somebody else."

I almost dropped my scissors. I asked, "What is it about her that drives you crazy?"

John gave a reply I'd heard at various times from all my male clients: meals were sporadic, the house wasn't clean, and his wife constantly nagged at him for help. When he finished with his list, I let John know that he wasn't going to find a woman who wasn't like that, especially if he didn't do his share.

Hey, keep the one you've got

I told him that every man or woman I have talked to has the same problem, he might as well keep the one he's got.

"Aw, come on, Sherri," he said. He left, but our conversation must have opened his eyes because that Saturday he and his wife both visited me at the salon after hours to discuss the ups and downs of marriage.

I bullied the two of them into going to a marriage counselor. It started out rough but eventually gave them both a new outlook on their marriage. After a year or so, John told me he was so thankful he still had his wife and little girl.

Thought I'd marry three times like my mom

"I used to think I would probably be married two or three times like my mom," he said. "I even got married with the idea that if it didn't work out, I could just get divorced."

THROUGH KID'S EYES

How many children of divorce think the same way? We all internalize what we see growing up, and we rely on our childhood interpretations of life to inform our choices as adults. If we grow up seeing parents or close friends divorce, we think that our relationships will eventually end that way too.

Children can't see the real cost of divorce, or truly understand the quality of their parent's lives after they've gone through divorce—or the quality of life for other couples that have worked out differences and remained together instead.

MYTH #3

Now let us examine myth #3:
Parents should not stay together just for the sake of the children.

Kids shackled to your problems

In the first place, anything parents do for the sake of the children is wonderful! More wonderful still would be not to force children to be shifted back and forth. Nor to force them to travel out of town because the court says they must. Nor to force stepparents and stepsiblings on them every time a remarriage occurs. Nor to force them into court to solve your problems.

After examining all the myths and their "real-life" flaws, the original marriage seems like the place to be.

Real mom loves kids best

Unfortunately, in most situations, no stepmother will love your children as much as their own mom does. From what I hear from my clients, totally loving stepmoms are few and far between.

Fix, not flee, an unhappy marriage

You should not stay in an unhappy marriage for the sake of the children. Instead, you should *fix* your unhappy marriage for the sake of the children and everyone else.

Happiness is a feeling, and feelings can be restored. Staying in what Dr. Liz Hale calls a "good-enough marriage" is better than a divorce. For the sake of the children, nothing is better than to show them not to give up and to work through their unhappiness until it turns to happiness. Nothing is better than showing your kids that having a lifelong relationship is possible for you and for them.

REMINDERS:

- Don't wait until you are divorced to realize that you love and want to be with your original wife after all.

- If you've ever been happy together, you can work to achieve happiness again.

- If you are fighting all the time while you're married, you will continue to fight after the divorce—only now you'll be fighting over the children. They will know that and think they are at fault.

NOTES

1. Linda J. Waite, et al., "Does Divorce Make People Happy? Findings from a Study of Unhappy Marriages," Institute for American Values, 2002.

CHAPTER 16

Costs: Part Two
CONTINUING COSTS OF DIVORCE

Nine-tenths of wisdom is being wise in time.

—Teddy Roosevelt

D ivorce is nothing to take lightly. It will cost you financially and emotionally, and it will cost your kids too. And sometimes during the extreme stress of the process, we make decisions that we will regret the rest of our lives.

Look into the future, beyond your immediate "getting out of here." What will happen to your

- Dad Time?
- Grandpa Time?
- Finances?
- Children?

Once you add children to your marriage, you have to take the question of whether to divorce with utmost seriousness. Children don't ask to be born, and it's your obligation to raise them as a family until they are grown.

DAD TIME WITH YOUR KIDS

Let's examine three issues before you dump the problems that are sending you to divorce court onto your children and make them their problems:

ISSUE #1: CUSTODY

(1) *How much time will you get with your kids in the perpetual shuffle between your home and your exes?*

You probably relish the times your young children come and jump in your arms or give you a cuddle before bed, or playing ball with them in the backyard. When you decide to get a divorce, the courts make iron-clad rules. Sometimes there is joint custody and sometimes there is sole custody.

Courts set visits

Even in joint custody one parent has physical custody. Most times it's the mother who has physical custody. The full-time custodian gets the kids all the time except for one day a week and every other weekend, for example. If you live at a distance that interferes with school attendance, weekdays are out, leaving you with every other weekend.

Where is home?

You will be spending a lot of your time driving to a pick-up point. You will see your children with suitcases in hand all the time, as if they don't really have a home. That's how they feel some times. So after the big run to hug their daddy, I would surmise that the rest of the weekend they are wondering why they can't be with their friends. This brings us to issue number two:

ISSUE #2: ANGER AND TEARS

(2) *How angry and retaliatory will your children be for you taking them away from their real mom? Away from their comfortable home and circle of friends? For turning their life upside down?*

Acting out

Anger and sadness are flip sides of the same coin when children start their suitcase life. They will be angry much of the time, and perhaps they will manifest their anger appropriately, but often they don't. They will lash out at anyone who gets in their way.

Blaming

Children blame the parent who left.

I had a client I will call Bob, who had a good reason to leave his marriage. There were years of infidelity and drugs. Even with all of that, he tried to make it work for the kids' sakes.

The counseling sessions were way too much for Jean, his wife. So she abruptly called a halt to the sessions and told him to leave. Bob did everything he could for the children, and yet the oldest son, Erin, ended up hating him and wouldn't speak to him for two years.

Finally after the long absence, Erin came around again and couldn't get enough of his dad. When he came in for a haircut, every other word was his dad and every other event had his dad's name attached. It seemed he was always trying to make up for lost time.

One day, Bob asked him, "Son, what did I do that was so wrong that you could hate me so much."

Erin's answer was, "You were the one who left." Then he added, "Do you realize how painful that was for me?"

Bob told me that before the divorce he did everything with Erin. They had been inseparable. The divorce would have been terribly painful for Erin.

Children also take turns defending the one they perceive as the culprit and blame the other spouse. I have clients who talk about one of their parents as if they were the devil himself. Then on the next trip for a haircut, the other parent gets the wrath.

Those big, unexpected hugs from your kids will be gone. Hearing your children's voices in the morning will be gone.

Missing friends more than dad

Children will become more and more aware that they are missing a party, game, or sleepovers with their friends because they must leave to visit dad. That "happy to see dad" grin might be only a momentary flash.

PAIN-FILLED STORY

I know an eleven-year-old girl who refused to go for visitations at all. The mother, to her credit, tried to talk her into it because she knew this little girl needed a relationship with her father. But the mom was not about to force her daughter, considering all the other stress the girl faced.

Dad could have taken the issue to court to force visits. But he decided that would be too expensive and that his daughter would hate him.

Hate him she did. The hate didn't manifest itself for a year and a half, but when it did, she blamed everybody. Not because anyone was at fault, only because she was in so much pain.

CONSIDER THE FOREVER PRICE

Make sure to keep those smiles and morning hugs in place, no matter what you have to do to stay together instead of divorcing.

WORST DIVORCE FALLOUT

Sam always had a wonderful relationship with his two kids when he was married. When Sam and his wife divorced, his ex relocated to a state far away and took their children with her.

Now it seemed the kids hated him. They refused to come for visits as the courts had stipulated. Several times Sam traveled across the continent to get a glimpse of his growing children, but to no avail. His ex refused to let him in, and the children sent messages that they wanted nothing to do with him.

Twenty lost years

Sam was bewildered. "What could I have done that was so bad that the children hate me so much?"

Twenty years passed before Will, his son, searched for and found Sam. Angry words spewed from his son's mouth: "Why didn't you want me? Where were you all of my life?"

Sam waited for his son to vent his hate and venom, and then he said, "Will, I want to show you something." He brought out a stack of "return to sender" unopened letters, all addressed to both his son and daughter, Sandy.

Sabotage

Will began to cry, "Why didn't you pay child support? You have no idea what a hard time we had."

Sam went to his office and retrieved a box with twenty years of returned checks. They were proof that he had paid his child support every month.

"How could Mom!" wailed Will. "She told us that you never wanted kids and that you wanted us 'bastards' out of your life."

How do you mend?

"Read the letters, Will," Sam said as he put his arm firmly across his son's shoulder. "I have loved and missed you and Sandy desperately. I never did give up. I knew the day would come that I would know the answers to all of this mess."

Will and Sandy are both trying to make up for lost time with their father. The relationship with their mom is a different story. They have not forgiven their mother for lying to them. They both say they will never speak to her again.

I hope for their sakes that they can learn to forgive her and have a relationship with both parents.

ISSUE #3: STEPPARENTS

(3) What will happen to your children when they don't like their new stepparent(s), which is typical? And how will you react?

Couch surfing

I was talking to Vicki, one of my clients. She said she was having problems with her son Tommy.

"Tommy wants to move out," she told me. "He has been staying with one friend or another. He just doesn't want to be home."

I asked her why.

Can't cope with stepfather

She said, "He and his stepfather have never gotten along. They are both very stubborn."

Her story was all too familiar. "Tommy never did forgive me for taking his father away. And then forcing another father on him."

"How does he feel about his real dad?" I asked.

Loves dad but not stepmom

"He really loves his dad." Vicki said, "And his dad has no idea about all the problems we've had. We are actually talking about sending Tommy to live with his dad." She hesitated for a moment and confided, "But his new wife doesn't like Tommy, and the feeling is mutual."

Familiar life-changing mistake

Then she admitted what I had heard often from other wives. "My first husband is a great guy. But he just never helped me when we were married. He was like having a third child. So I left."

She had that forlorn look on her face as if she had made a huge mistake.

* * *

GRANDPA TIME WITH YOUR OWN

Consider your future with your grandchildren before you jump ship.

TALE OF AN ADULT CHILD OF DIVORCE

One of my clients said, "I am sixty-five years old and my parents have been divorced for thirty years. Not once has my dad been to a birthday party or a ball game or anything where his grandkids are concerned."

"Never?" I said. "Why not?"

Tentacles of pain reach new generation

She said, "Because my mom and my dad's second wife can't be in the same room at the same time." She continued, "Sherri, my kids and grandkids have achieved so much, and he doesn't even know it. He has never been to a high school graduation. He hasn't even been to Josh's college graduation where he was valedictorian."

The pain of divorce lasts through your children's adulthood and spreads its tentacles into the next generation.

FIGHTS OVER WHO GETS TIME WITH GRANDKIDS

As the years roll by, it's likely you will spend time fighting with your ex-spouse over who will get a weekend with the grandchildren. You will argue with your second (or third) spouse over whose set of grandchildren is more important to see this holiday or this month. Best wishes trying to explain to your own grandchildren why Grandpa and Grandma can't visit together.

THE LUCKY ONES

The couples that stayed together and worked on their marriages, however, can be having the time of their lives with their grandchildren. Neither grandparent has to pretend to enjoy kids he or she doesn't know—they both worship the same group of children. This brings a certain ease and joy to your lives, and it makes life easier for the kids too. This is your reward for making your relationships work—a reward surpassing all your expectations.

* * *

YOUR FINANCES AT JEOPARDY

The only thing financially certain about divorce is that your bank account will gradually become your lawyer's bank account. Nothing is free in the legal system. And don't expect the legal system to be fair.

DESTITUTE WIVES—AND HUSBANDS

You hear stories of men divorcing and impoverishing their wives out of spite. You may not hear the stories of men made similarly destitute.

An older male friend of mine was taken to the cleaners. He lost his equity in the family house and land that he had worked two jobs to buy, build, and keep. Now he lives month to month on rage and Social Security.

I know of many other wallet-wrenching outcomes.

DREAMS IN SHAMBLES

Another man told me, "If I had still been married, I would have had my house paid for. My business was just becoming successful. Now

I have a house payment on a new house. I'm living payday to payday after paying child support for three girls and all the extracurricular activities they have in school. My ex was supposed to split the costs . . .

"I've lived two years in limbo. I never see my kids as much as I want. My business is back to square one, and I have to start over."

There are so many good reasons to fix a once-happy marriage and make it work again for you and your family, no matter what you have to do.

POVERTY FORCED ON YOUR CHILDREN

Whether poverty is forced on either spouse, it is your children (or grandchildren)—who did not divorce either parent—who will be the most vulnerable victims. Think! How will being raised in poverty (yours or hers) shape your children's lives?

WORK EATS UP PARENT TIME

Although this is an example of a divorced wife, it could happen to your children:

After divorce, the ex-wife had to work full time and overtime. Her responsibilities with the children magnified because now she was the sole parent in her household, and her children struggled after the divorce.

She couldn't be there for them when they needed her because she was always working. Gone was the attendance at school functions, the hugs and greetings when the kids got home from school. Her children acted as if they had been abandoned and resented her for moving them from their big, beautiful home into "the dump," as they called their apartment.

* * *

CHILDREN CHANGED FOREVER

When children are dragged into a divorce, their emotions are split in half. Children never stop trying to decide who is right and who is wrong on any given situation. They seem to want to be the savior of the one whom everyone is mad at no matter what the reason. Sibling fights erupt over who is on whose side at different intervals.

SUICIDAL REACTION TO PARENTS' DIVORCE

Children are more vulnerable than you think. Psychologist Dr. Liz Hale says divorce is "emotional suicide in many cases."

I interviewed quite a few children about their parents' divorce. One boy didn't want to talk about it, so I had him draw some pictures, especially of his hobby of riding motorcycles.

Revealed in art

He was a pretty good little artist. He drew five pictures that were quite impressive. The sixth picture was of a skyscraper, complete with windows from top to bottom.

On the top of the skyscraper he drew a kid on a motorcycle driving across the top of the building. In order for the motorcycle to be moving he drew a number of bikes and then drew movement between them.

Deadly motorcycle ride

The bike crossed the top of the building and kept going when it got to the edge. Then it fell and fell until it hit the ground.

As I looked at the picture, I asked him, "Who is that on the motorcycle?"

He said, "That's me." He was very matter of fact.

I said, "Why don't you draw a great big swimming pool so when the motorcycle falls you won't get hurt."

Boy sees no alternative

He drew an elaborate swimming pool. I walked away for a minute, thinking all was well. However, when I went back I noticed the motorcycle in motion again. This time it splashed into the water and flew up to the windows high up at the middle of the skyscraper.

What he said next sent chills down my spine.

He said, "See, even if the swimming pool is there, I fly into the building smashing through the windows and I die anyway."

He walked away as if nothing unusual had been said.

In a coffin

Just so you don't think this is a unique story, here's another example:

A little girl whose parents had filed for divorce came in for a haircut.

She told me her parents were trying to work things out. I found out later this was only her wishful thinking.

I asked her, "How would you feel if your parents got back together."

She became extremely animated and said, "It would be like being dead in a coffin and then coming back to life again."

ADULT CHILDREN LEARN BY YOUR EXAMPLE

What about a plan to stay together until the kids are out of the house? That's cheating!

Adult children still learn by your example, and a divorce will still confuse them. They will see you and your spouse fighting longer instead of fixing your relationship. It will still hurt them. It will still make them question their own level of commitment in relationships. It will still force them to deal with stepparents. And it will force their children to deal with step-grandparents, some of whom just might not like them.

LEARNING TOO LATE

What a significant number of couples have discovered, too late of course, was that staying and fixing their marriage would be a lot easier, less stressful, and more fulfilling than to give it all up to live a separate life from your children. No one knows the horrors of divorce until they get there, or until they have a close loved one go through it.

REMINDERS:

- Nothing is free in the legal system, and don't expect the legal system to be fair.

- Think beyond "now" to the future: Your Dad time will shrink. Your Grandpa time will be divided or unsure.

- Divorce is wallet-wrenching. Your bank account will gradually become your lawyer's bank account; what's left will be eaten up by alimony and child-support payments and travel to have your children shuttle between homes.

- Divorce costs your children's future as well: They blame themselves and often act out, become manipulating or suicidal. Stepparents rarely love your child like their own.

CHAPTER 17

GOLDEN RULES IF YOU ARE ALREADY DIVORCED

Do something every day that you don't want to do. This is the golden rule for acquiring the habit of doing your duty without pain.

—Mark Twain

Here are three Golden Rules to live by for the sake of your children if you are already divorced. If you are separated, the time is ideal to implement these strategies for a better long-term outcome.

1. ALLOW CHILDREN TO LOVE THEIR OTHER PARENT. Remember that you and your wife divorced each other. Your children did not divorce their mother—or you.

2. SPEAK NO EVIL. Do not put down their mother in front of your children. Always speak respectfully. No matter how angry you are or how many grievances you would like to proclaim, she is their mother. Your ex-wife should also abide by the "speak no evil" rule.

3. DISARMAMENT PACT. Do not abuse your children by using them as weapons against your ex. Do not force them to take sides. Your arguments with your wife should be just that. Your children should never be caught in the middle.

LETTER TO EX

One of my clients wrote this short note to his ex-wife after their divorce and wanted to know what I thought. I was very proud of him. His points exemplify the Golden Rules listed above.

We need to work together for the benefit of our children.

Our daughters have been kicked in the stomach. They need the love of both of their parents more than ever right now.

Our daughters need both of us in their lives, now more than ever. I am asking you to please in no way allow them to disrespect or avoid me. We don't have to get along, but you owe it to them to support their father. This means you and I should be on the same page in everything we say and do. They need to have the same rules and expectations from both of us about school, personal conduct, and rules.

We should also come to an agreement as to whether they should be in therapy. They need to be able to sort out all the turmoil they are going through. They need to know that both of their parents love them more than life.

We need to be collaborators, not competitors. Let's make a plan we can both agree on so our daughters don't suffer. All that matters is that we put our girls before everything else, because if we don't, it will be at their expense and ultimately yours and mine.

* * *

IT'S ABOUT OUR CHILDREN, NOT US

Bruce and Shelly met and married after their divorces. Because they each had custody of their own children, all seven kids lived together most of the time.

At first, all the children were having a hard time and had been diagnosed with post-traumatic stress disorder (PTSD). They were getting bad grades in school. They were sad all the time and initially not willing to accept their new siblings.

Doing the unthinkable

When the ex-wife came to the house, Shelly invited her in. This made her new husband, Bruce, irate.

He told Shelly that he didn't want his ex-wife anywhere near him. Shelly said, "This isn't about us. It's about our children."

Taking the high road

Because he loved his children, Bruce eventually also took the high road, even becoming friendly with Shelly's ex-husband. The positive transformation in the children was amazing.

Profound thanks from their children

Now their children thank them all the time because they know how much effort it took. Ironically, however, acting kindly to the children's other biological parents has made Shelly and Bruce happier too.

* * *

SPEAK NO EVIL

I have a granddaughter whose parents divorced. I always was extra careful to never say anything bad about her dad. I would always ask her how he was and to tell him I said "Hi."

One day about two years into the divorce there was a flare up of turmoil and it was evident that the dad had been the culprit.

My granddaughter began to tell the story, and she was blaming her mom.

Like an idiot, I jumped in and said, "Wait a minute, don't you remember what happened? This wasn't your mom's fault. Your dad . . ."

Granddaughter's correction

She stopped me in my tracks and said, "Grandma, I don't appreciate you saying bad things about my dad."

She had caught me. I said, "Do you realize that this is the first time I have ever said anything bad about your dad the whole time he and your mom have been divorced?"

She was still determined, "I don't care, and you shouldn't ever do it."

I agreed. I promised her I never would.

CHILDREN TAKE CRITICISM PERSONALLY

When you talk about the child's parents you are talking about that child's DNA. Children take it personally. No matter how bad you think your ex-spouse is, even if you are right, that child will always love her. Think about it.

REMINDERS:

- Allow your children to love their mother. They did not divorce your wife—or you.

- Never put down their mother in front of your children.

- Do not abuse your children by using them as weapons against your ex. Do not force them to take sides.

CHAPTER 18

SUCCESS STORIES

THIRD MARRIAGE AT 24

"I am on my third marriage," said a man at one of my book signings after waiting until no one else was around my table. "I am only twenty-four, and I think I am going to lose this one too.

His shoulders slumped. "I always thought it was their fault, but now I am beginning to wonder."

Searching for help

He checked to make sure the coast was still clear. "Do you think this book will help me?"

"Tell me who does most of the housework at your house?" I asked.

"She does most of the housework, but I help her sometimes," he sheepishly answered.

"Does she work?" I asked.

He answered quickly, "Yes, she works two jobs, but I make the most money."

Respect for each other

"It doesn't matter who makes the most money. It matters who is the most tired. But most of all it matters how much respect you both have for each other, which means you must share everything."

He didn't wince; he didn't argue. It seemed he desperately wanted to save his marriage.

To him and his wife

He bought the book and had me sign it to him and his wife.

I told him that he couldn't just buy the book and hope something good comes out of it. We both laughed as I explained that he should read the whole book (hopefully with or to his wife).

As he left he said, "I will, and thanks so much for talking to me."

His results

I did a few other signings elsewhere in the state, and then I was back at that same store. After an hour, this same young man came bouncing in and came straight to my table.

"Everything is wonderful," he said. He seemed so happy. He didn't even care who was listening this time.

Points for doing something

"First of all, my wife was so happy that I actually bought this book in order to save our marriage. Then she was more than happy to read it with me."

He confessed, "I didn't even know that I was supposed to do all those things. She never told me." Then he continued, "It seems that housework was the biggest part of our problem. So we went to the back of the book and picked permanent jobs."

Now she recognized my fit-it stuff too

"You know, Sherri," he said, "She had been so mad about doing all the housework that she said she just took for granted the fix-it stuff I do." Then apologetically he said, "Don't get me wrong, that is nothing compared with what she does on a regular basis." Smiling he said, "But I love how she recognizes it now."

No more twenty-four-hour tension

"Has it been a big adjustment for you?" I asked.

"Absolutely not," he said with gusto. "The extra work I do around the house is nothing compared to the tension I felt twenty-four hours a day, wondering why she was so angry, wondering if she was going to walk out on me like the other two had." He seemed so happy. "I can't believe what your book has done."

Then he turned to the other people who were standing by my table and said, "You need to buy Sherri's book. It is the most wonderful thing that has ever happened to me."

* * *

FROM A PSYCHOLOGIST

A couple came into the therapist's office wanting help to get through their divorce. They had little children and wanted it to go as smoothly as possible. They had already filed for divorce and could see how it was affecting the children.

The therapist said, "I have a book here that I want you to read."

It was my book.

Read this book, and then we'll talk

Then she said, "If you promise to go home and read this book from cover to cover, I promise you I will help you through your divorce."

The couple came back, holding hands. They had canceled their divorce proceedings and wanted to thank the therapist for saving their marriage and their children.

* * *

ADVICE ECHOES IN HEAD

One of the men I interviewed later told me he even benefited from our discussion:

"I now automatically think of your words of wisdom when my wife and I discuss any family chore. One person SHOULDN'T be doing it all.

Any excuse . . . no more

"Men can, and do, use any excuse why not to clean the table . . . or do the dishes. Excuses, like 'I worked hard all day.' Or, 'I have something I need to finish.' Or, 'I have a church calling to get to.' I am no different. But I get it now. Just getting up and doing it not only feels good, but also sets a good example for the kids. And also often leads to intimacy. She feels appreciated. She's not so exhausted."

* * *

WIFE READS BOOK TO HUSBAND

A client read my first book to her husband.

He was dumbfounded at learning of the unfairness at home.

She came home from work and he had everything in the house shining and he had a dinner on the table. She was more than flabbergasted. What he said to her really made her smile, and she couldn't wait to get in for her haircut to tell me.

Do me proud

He had said, "I bet Sherri would really be proud of me, don't you think?"

I loved it, especially since I hardly knew him. He also told her he had been checking the back of the book in anticipation of making things permanent. Yes! Another saved marriage, one couple at a time!

* * *

WIN-WIN TESTIMONIAL FROM MALE READER

"We all fall unthinkingly into the traditional roles we grew up in where household tasks fell heavily on women. But there is something wrong with women being completely responsible for housework. It is wrong for my wife to be expected to do it all and for me to only help.

"Sherri gives a BRILLIANT solution. I have never heard a better explanation of why help is not helpful. She said that the only way to fix the problem is for a man to take permanent ownership of tasks.

Rewards from taking charge of tasks

"Once I established that solution in my mind, I didn't have to be stressed over what my wife expects of me.

"We men know there are things that we want that we have trouble relaying to our wives or getting fulfillment. I found that by making my wife's life easier, it is also a great way of getting my sexual needs met. What a great trade-off!"

CHAPTER 19

NOT MARRIED?
I HOPE YOU TAKE
THAT CHANCE

Everyone says love hurts but that is not true. Loneliness hurts,
envy hurts. Everyone gets these things confused with love. But in reality,
love is the only thing in the world that covers up all pain and makes
someone feel wonderful again.

—Dr. Wayne Dyer

I've heard men say they are never getting married because it's just too much trouble. They fear marrying the wrong person and then having to go through a divorce. I think these are the first generations with so many peers who have grown up with bad divorces.

As a single guy, do you hear and are you convinced by all the bad stuff that happens in a marriage? Do you ever hear about the powerfully exhilarating times that make marriage worthwhile?

If you talk with another man who is going through or has just gotten a divorce, be alert for two things at play here.

- (1) **Hey, it wasn't his fault**. His ex is no good and here are all the stories to prove it. Good times? He doesn't remember any.
- (2) **Misery loves company**. He wants a buddy with whom to share his grief, to become equally down on women so that he

can vent unrestrained. Heap on stories of child custody fights, courtroom drama, money down the drain, and not being able to see his kids as much as he wants to—he's going full throttle.

IT'S ABOUT DIVORCE, STUPID

If you wait around long enough, what you will discover in most cases is that it wasn't the marriage that was so bad. It was that two people who probably had a pretty good marriage, decided to end it without having the faintest idea what they were in for. All the negative talk you are hearing about marriage isn't about marriage at all. It's about divorce.

POWER OF POSITIVE THINKING

This doesn't have to be the outcome. Instead of worrying that your marriage might not work out, why don't you get married and make sure you do everything to make sure it works? If you start thinking positively in the beginning, your chances are enormous of living with your love "until death do you part."

TIPS FOR A LONG MARRIAGE

I cut the following piece of genius out of a newspaper and have had it in my wallet for a few years. Based on my experience, I believe every word of it:

[A couple] said the secrets to their successful 70-year marriage include remembering a few bits of wisdom:

- Everyone has faults: *"We decided to put up with each other's faults, rather than find new ones."*
- Stick it out for the kids: *"Divorce is so hard on children, so we never wanted to go through it."*
- Jobs at home: *"We decided to divide up the household chores, from paying bills to maintaining the yard, and we do our jobs in our own way."*
- We meant it when we said our vows—*to have and to hold, from this day forward, for better or for worse, for richer and poorer, in sickness and in health, until death do us part."*
- Let the "disagreements" go. *Don't hold on to grudges; life is too short.*[1]

I would also add, "You can't always be right and have a happy marriage at the same time." (see chapter 12)

FRIGHTENED BY "WHAT IFS"

When you are young, sometimes your fears are a lot worse than reality.

Merrill, a friend of mine, married a great gal named Ellie. They were planning on having a large family, until his sister had a baby who was born with Down syndrome named Jenny. Both Merrill and Ellie panicked and decided that they were not going to chance that happening to them. Merrill had a vasectomy.

Reluctantly, they did become godparents to Jenny.

Merrill's sister had three more perfectly normal children.

Rewards missed

As the children grew, Merrill and Ellie grew closer to Jenny, as did everyone touched by her. She had such a glow about her that nobody could resist loving her. Jenny became Merrill and Ellie's favorite out of all their nieces.

Merrill and Ellie both have grieved endlessly over their decision to forego a family of their own because they are sure now they made a mistake.

They were not willing to take that chance.

MARRIAGE CAN WORK

When you find yourself falling in love with someone, there's usually a reason why you love that person. If done the right way, as outlined in this book, the love you have in the beginning can grow over time and become better than you could ever possibly imagine. Two willing partners can mold together. Go extra where she lacks, and allow her to thrive where you lack. Don't assume you always have to be the powerhouse, or feel threatened by her capabilities. When you're married, you're a team.

REMINDERS:

- When you hear bad things about a marriage, it's probably about a fight. When good things are happening in a marriage, husbands (or wives) have no need to vent.

- Misery loves company. When a buddy is going through a divorce, he wants you to think marriage and women are awful. That way you'll be on his side.

- It wasn't the marriage that was so bad. Instead, it was the divorce.

NOTES

1. Jennifer Sanchez, "Couple, Married 70 Years, Can't Get Enough of Each Other," *Salt Lake Tribune*, January 2, 2009.

A MESSAGE TO WOMEN WHO WON'T GIVE UP CONTROL: LET HIM DO IT HIS WAY

Occasionally when a husband is ready to do his share of householder tasks, neither spouse experiences joy because the wife is unwilling to give up her control.

In my "gloves off" approach, I call such a wife a culturally stagnant specimen of a resentful, angry, hateful, guilt-ridden woman who would rather do it all *and* still be angry all the time. Angry and hateful because she buys into society's outdated message that she would be a failure if she didn't do it all.

CAN YOU BELIEVE IT?

My client Cindy came in the salon all the time with complaints about her husband. It might surprise you what they were.

She said, "You should see Gary. After he eats his breakfast, he rinses all the dishes off. He washes the table off. He squirts out the sink." Then she rolled her eyes and almost shouted, "But he won't put the dishes in the dishwasher!"

She had more complaints: "He showers and then he washes the

shower curtain off, washes the tub, and puts everything back in its place. Then he wipes up the floor when it's wet."

RIGHTEOUS OUTRAGE

I didn't have long to wait for the "bad" thing he must have done.

"But he doesn't take the time to close the shower curtain," she said in righteous outrage.

In shock, I countered, "Do you have any idea how many women would give their eye teeth to have a man do the things that Gary does?"

I think she is a lost cause. And she is in her third, very wobbly marriage.

* * *

HE IS FINALLY TAKING CHARGE

One of my clients loves her husband very much and knows instinctively that she is at fault for not letting go.

She was telling me that after thirty-five years of her husband doing nothing around the house, he is finally taking charge.

She said, "Sherri, how do I get rid of the resentment and anger that has been built up for years?"

Accumulated anger

I said, "Are you still angry with him even though he is pulling his weight?"

She said, "I've got so much anger from the past that I want to jump on him when he does anything, because he doesn't do it to my expectations or specifications."

Neat freak

From past conversations, I knew she was a neat freak. I said, "Do you know what a gift he just gave you? You had better straighten yourself up before his cooperation is a thing of the past."

I rolled over her spluttering. "You must (1) forget the past and realize that he was as much in the dark as you were as to who was supposed to do domestic work. Then you can shed your anger. (2) You can surely find areas in the home where you can be OK if he does it his way. There are lots of corners, there are lots of hidden places, there's going to the store, ironing his own clothes. The list goes on."

Can't have it both ways

She sat there speechless. I continued, "You have to either do that or take back all the householder responsibilities. This time, however, you can't be angry or resentful toward him. This time you will have only yourself to blame. When retirement comes, he will be the only one retiring."

She stared silently into an appalling future.

Only yourself to blame

I added this cruel reminder, "Then when he is retired and you are still waiting on him and doing all the domestic work so your house will stay immaculate, you can blame yourself. Then you can say, 'at least he tried, but I wouldn't let it happen'."

I added, "Now that you are aware of the cold facts, you are the master of your own destiny."

Happy life with happy husband—big winner

We talked for a while longer. She ended up admitting how unimportant it was to have an immaculate house. Compared to having a happy life with a happy husband—an immaculate house loses hands down.

APPENDIX B

THE FAIR MARRIAGE CONTRACT

PROPOSED CONTRACT

The FAIR Marriage Contract

TO BE NEGOTIATED BY BOTH PARTIES

Permission granted to photocopy
© Sherri Mills 2013
THE FAIR MARRIAGE CONTRACT

THE FAIR MARRIAGE CONTRACT

It is the intention of this contract to effectively guide balanced and efficient operations of a household and at the same time provide against the workload abuse and unfair treatment of any householder.

The major purpose for negotiations between male and female householders is to set forth expectations and obligations so as to promote peaceful and loving relationships between parties at all levels. The goal is a sustained effort by all parties to achieve a loving home and smooth-running operations. The balancing of chores aims to eliminate non-performance caused by overload of female householder duties, resulting in occupational illness, extreme fatigue, and/or resentment.

Eliminating unfair and unhealthy working conditions would automatically remove overburden and occupational health hazards and yield stability to household operations, reduce emotional problems for all householders, improve communications between adult householders, and increase mutual respect.

HIGHLIGHTS OF PROPOSED EXPECTATIONS

IV. Classifications and Responsibilities

V. Coverage of Compensation

VI. Preservation of Health and Safety Rights

VII. Personal and Sick Days

VIII. Holidays and Vacations

IX. Discrimination

X. Settlement of Disputes

XI. Addendum: Chore lists for selecting

I

CLASSIFICATIONS

1. Female householder at home full time.

2. Female householder working outside the home full time.

RESPONSIBILITIES

to be done or delegated by . . .

1. Female householder at home full time:

    a. Housekeeping

    b. Shopping

    c. Cooking

    d. Laundry

    e. Nurse

    f. Chauffer

    g. Social Secretary

    h. Managing Children's Affairs

    i. Record Keeping

(NOTE: These and other chores to be shared with all household members on weekends and after school or after male householder's job as negotiated in this contract—VIII Addendum.)

2. Female householder working outside the home full time:

SHARE ALL RESPONSIBILITIES with all household members as negotiated in this contract—VIII Addendum.

II

COVERAGE OF COMPENSATIONS

1. COMPENSATIONS FOR FEMALE HOUSEHOLDER AT HOME FULL TIME:

   a. Weekly allowance for personal use.

   b. Integrate housework among all householders, taking male householder's full-time job restrictions into consideration.

2. COMPENSATIONS FOR FEMALE HOUSEHOLDER WORKING OUTSIDE THE HOME FULL TIME:

   a. If householder duties are shared 50/50, the employed female householder shares her income with the household and is a full partner in all financial and domestic projects.

   b. If all householder duties are done or delegated by employed female householder, a significant portion of money coming from the female householder's full-time job shall be earmarked for hiring out some or all of the housekeeping duties, as the female householder sees necessary for creating balance and leisure in her own life.

III

PRESERVATION OF HEALTH AND SAFETY RIGHTS

1. Female and male householders will alternate obligations of being on call 24 hours a day, 365 days a year.

2. Alternating on-call obligations will result in female householder's freedom to make decisions without first making arrangements for the kids and household to be taken care of, as the entire burden will no longer rest on her shoulders.

IV

PERSONAL AND SICK LEAVE

1. When either the female or male householder is ill, all duties will be taken over completely by other householders until sick householder recuperates.

   a. All duties will be performed so ill householder doesn't have double duty when she or he recuperates.

V

HOLIDAYS AND VACATIONS

1. All holidays should be for the enjoyment of all householders with preparations and cleanup shared by all householders.

2. Any work required in preparation for, during, or returning from vacations should be shared mutually by all householders.

VI

DISCRIMINATION

1. No person shall be discriminated against.

   a. No person shall be discriminated against on basis of wages earned.

   b. No person shall be coerced into a job unsuitable for his or her skills or time constraints.

   c. No person shall be put down. Put-downs *from either party* shall result in said complainer doing the at-home worker's duties for a full weekend.

VII

SETTLEMENT OF DISPUTES

1. Male and female householder may choose the means best suited for him or her in settling disputes, whether orally or in writing.

   a. Oral dispute settlement will be used to express oneself verbally ONLY if one is best suited to do so. And only if one is calm enough to discuss the matter without violence or put-downs.

   b. Written dispute settlement will be used to express oneself if one is verbally intimidated or if one is best suited to express oneself on paper.

2. VERBAL ABUSE BY EITHER PARTY IS NOT ACCEPTABLE.

Signature of Female Householder   Date

Signature of Male Householder   Date

Fair practices to all household members must result so an agreement can be ratified.

This is not a legal contract and must be taken to the appropriate parties to be legalized. The author of this contract is not liable for any outcome that may result in the signing of said contract.

VIII

ADDENDUM TO THE CONTRACT

The List of Householder Chores to be divided fairly among all householders.

1. Chore division will be spread fairly among all parties while taking time constraints into consideration.

2. Chores assigned will be taken on as the full responsibility of the signing householder for life or until a time of further negotiation.

HOUSEHOLDER
CHORE LISTS

I n this section you will find day-by-day, week-by-week, and month-by-month lists of responsibilities to be shared. Sit your entire family down together and have everyone choose the chores he or she will take on permanently. Be sure you train your children to do the chores they pick, and be sure you don't allow a child to pick a chore that's too difficult or one that's inappropriate.

If you believe you can negotiate a realignment of householder duties with your fellow householders, photocopy just the chore lists.

RESPONSIBLE FOR SELF

If you'd like every member of your household to take on a certain chore for themselves (packing for vacations, for example), just write "Individual" next to that chore.

FINANCIAL CHORES

In many cases, these jobs go together in one lump, or you risk having your finances become haphazard. You can also take on these chores together, figure out who is the more responsible when it comes to paying bills on time, or determine who is more skilled at investments, insurance, and other money matters.

It's essential that both partners know what is going on with their money, however, so if you don't take on the money chore together, be sure to update your partner on the state of your finances and savings every few months.

Taking on financial chores counts as seven chores in our household: sorting and answering mail, paying bills, making deposits, arranging for financial gifts, paying children's school dues, managing investments, and updating partner on money matters. Break down all the parts of money matters as they occur in your life and count each part as one chore.

CHORES FOR CAMPING (OR OTHER RECREATION)

My family loves to go camping. The chores for camping are so different than the chores one might have on another kind of trip that we had to have a separate chore list for it. I include it for you to photocopy if you need it. Be sure to leave it out if your family doesn't camp or modify it to fit the type of recreation your family pursues.

Does your family like to snowshoe on Sundays? Are you do-it-yourselfers who love to spend a weekend building a closet or porch? Use the camping list as a guide and list the necessary chores for any activity your family does regularly, then divide those up. You'll find a blank chart for doing this at the end of the camping chore list.

CHORES FOR VERY YOUNG CHILDREN

To make very young children feel included—and to let them know that living in a house is everyone's responsibility—let even your youngest children pick an appropriate chore from the list. Daily chores for very young children are listed separately. These chores are actually the things you and the child have to do together every day: eat breakfast, put the bowl in the sink or dishwasher, brush teeth, and so on. If you turn these daily habits into little chores, your child will learn to do chores from the start. You'll be able to take this time to train the child to clean up after herself in all she does. She not only brushes her teeth (or has them brushed for her), but she puts her toothbrush back in its holder and wipes the edge of the sink. I have known people to use this list with babies, telling them everything they are doing as Mommy or Daddy does it. As soon as the child begins to toddle, she has heard that you put pajamas in the hamper a hundred times, and she's fully prepared to do it herself.

PERIODIC CHORES

As you write the name of the householder who'll be taking on each periodic chore, you'll need to decide when some of these chores must be done. You can write the date the chore must be completed, or you can write a deadline the chore must be completed by. (Example: The ovens will be cleaned by January 15, April 15, July 15 and November 15 each year, or they must be cleaned on January 15, April 15, July 15 and November 15.) If you list specific dates, be sure to leave leeway in case of emergencies, changes of plans, and special events.

A LAST NOTE

Photocopy everything you need and make changes according to your lifestyle.

CHORE LIST FOR TODDLERS AND YOUNG CHILDREN

This entire list is intended for one child to use every day. You can help the child put a check mark or small sticker next to each chore every day.

	Mon	Tue	Wed	Thu	Fri	Sat	Sun
Wake up politely							
Eat breakfast							
Put dish in sink or dishwasher							
Brush teeth							
Put toothbrush away							
Dry edge of sink							
Choose clothes							
Get dressed							
Put pajamas in drawer or hamper							
Make bed							
Eat lunch							
Put dish in sink or dishwasher							
Eat dinner							
Put dish in sink or dishwasher							
Take bath							
Empty bathtub							

Put on pajamas							
Put clothes in hamper							
Pick up toys							
Read bedtime story							

DAILY CHORES

Each family member should list his or her name next to the chores he or she will take on permanently—either daily, weekends, or weekdays.

	Mon	Tue	Wed	Thu	Fri	Sat	Sun
Waking everyone up							
Making beds							
Fixing breakfast							
Washing breakfast dishes/cleaning kitchen							
Getting everyone lunch or lunch money							
Fixing supper or bringing home takeout							
Washing supper dishes or cleaning up takeout mess							
Vacuuming							
Taking garbage to garbage can							
Caring for family pets including cleanup							
Sweep floors							
After-school talks with children and monitoring homework							
Bathing and dressing toddlers							
Getting clothes ready for next day							
Getting children to school or babysitter							
Picking up children							

Driving children to extracurricular activities							

WEEKLY CHORES

Each family member should list his or her name next to the chores he or she will take on permanently and do once weekly. You can write the day of the week you agree the chore will be done, or you can agree on a deadline. (*Example: The chore must be done by Sunday night at 7:00 p.m.*).

Upkeep of sprinkler system	
Mowing lawn	
Watering lawn	
Pulling weeds	
Watering plants	
Sorting clothes	
Washing clothes	
Putting away clothes	
Stripping beds and washing sheets	
Taking garbage out	
Taking garbage can to curb	
Ironing clothes	
Taking inventory and shopping for new clothes	
Polishing furniture	
Vacuuming	
Sweeping wood or tile floors	
Mopping wood or tile floors	
Dusting	
Cleaning tub or shower	

Cleaning toilet	
Picking up clutter	
Planning menu	
Buying groceries	

PERIODIC CHORES

Each family member should list his or her name next to the chores he or she will take on permanently.

Cleaning ovens	
Defrosting freezer	
Cleaning out refrigerator	
Shampooing carpets	
Washing walls and baseboards	
Cleaning cupboards	
Cleaning closets	
Washing interior windows	
Washing exterior windows	
Maintaining automobiles internally (engine)	
Maintaining automobiles externally (cleaning)	
Cleaning garage	
Responding to plumbing problems	
Responding to electrical problems	
Responding to appliance problems	
Maintaining heating and cooling systems	
Maintaining house exterior (paint, gutters, and so on)	
Roofing or arranging for roofer	
Doing interior construction projects	
Doing exterior construction projects	
Shoveling snow	
Planting annual flowers	
Trimming hedges	
Maintaining soil (fertilizing)	

Taking children to doctor	
Taking children to dentist	
Taking children for haircuts	

CHORES FOR HOLIDAYS

Each family member should list his or her name next to the chores he or she will take on permanently.

Preparation for children's birthdays:	
Buy presents	
Buy or make cake	
Plan party	
Buy groceries	
Buy decorations	
Send party invitations (or make calls)	
Host party	
Clean up after party	
Preparation for Thanksgiving:	
Buy groceries	
Send invitations (or make calls)	
Cook dinner	
Cook desserts	
Clean up after dinner	
Preparation for Winter holiday:	
String lights (decorate exterior)	
Decorate interior	
Buy presents	
Wrap presents	
Send holiday cards	
Send invitations (or make calls)	
Buy groceries	
Cook dinner	
Cook desserts (bake cookies)	
Arrange for travel	
Arrange for hosting guests	

CHORES FOR HOLIDAYS
AND OTHER SPECIAL EVENTS

CHORES FOR HOLIDAYS
AND OTHER SPECIAL EVENTS

CHORES FOR VACATIONS
AND WEEKEND GETAWAYS

Each family member should list his or her name next to the chores he or she will take on permanently.

Planning the vacation	
Making arrangements and reservations	
Preparing clothes	
Packing suitcases	
Packing children's play toys	
Getting children dressed and out the door	
Unpacking and washing clothes	
Putting everything away	

PACKING FOR CAMPING (OR OTHER RECREATION)

Each family member should list his or her name next to the chores he or she will take on permanently.

Pack gear (*list individual items*)	
Plan menu	
Shop for groceries	
Pack food	
Pack clothes	
Prepare camp trailer or vehicle	

CHORES WHILE CAMPING (OR OTHER RECREATION)

Cooking or preparing breakfast	
Cleaning up after breakfast	
Cooking or preparing lunch	

Cleaning up after lunch	
Cooking or preparing dinner	
Cleaning up after dinner	

CHORES AFTER CAMPING (OR OTHER RECREATION)

Unpacking equipment	
Unpacking clothing	
Cleaning the camp trailer or vehicle	
Washing clothing	
Putting clean clothing away	
Cleaning equipment	
Putting equipment away	
Putting food away	

CHORES ASSOCIATED WITH BABIES AND TODDLERS

Each family member should list his or her name next to the chores he or she will take on permanently.

Bathing and dressing babies in the morning	
Bathing baby at night	
Changing diapers during the day	
Changing diapers at night	

Feeding baby during the day	
Feeding baby at night	
Getting baby down for daytime naps	
Getting baby down for bed	
Getting up at night with baby	
Bathing baby at night	
Holding and comforting baby when cranky or sick	
Taking baby to doctor	
Holding or keeping baby occupied when partner does chore	

CHORES FOR MANAGING HOUSEHOLD FINANCES

One adult family member should list his or her name next to the financial chores and take them on permanently. It's good to discuss who best does each chore or group of chores. One person may be responsible for most or all of these chores.

Sorting and answering mail	
Paying bills	
Making deposits at the bank	
Arranging for gifts or money for weddings, birthdays, bereavement, etc.	
Paying for children's school fees	
Managing investments	
Updating partner on money matters	
Record keeping	
Tax preparation or gathering and delegating to professional	

Use this blank chart for any other tasks that you need to divide among householders.

CHORES FOR _____

BIBLIOGRAPHY

Betcher, William, M. D., and Robie Macauley, *The Seven Basic Quarrels of Marriage* (New York: Ballantine Books, 1990).

Boyack, Marrilee Brown, *Strangling Your Husband Is Not an Option* (Salt Lake City: Deseret Book, 2006).

Carnegie, Dale, *How to Stop Worrying and Start Living.* (New York: Pendaflex Corp., 1975)

"Court TV Editors and The American Lawyer," *The Court TV Cradle to Grave Legal Survival Guide* (New York: Little, Brown, 1995).

Dyer, Wayne W., *The Sky Is the Limit* (New York: Simon and Schuster, 1980).

Dyer Wayne W., *Staying on the Path* (Carson, CA: Hay House, 1995)

Hilliard, Laurie Lovejoy & Sharon Lovejoy Autry, *Mom and Loving It* (Minneapolis: Bethany House, 2005).

Jampolsky, G. Gerald, *Love Is Letting go of Fear* (Berkeley, CA: Celestial Arts, 1997).

Kushner, Harold S., *When Bad Things Happen to Good People* (New York: Schocken Books, 1981).

Losoncy, Lewis E., *Turning People On* (Englewood Cliffs, NJ: Prentice Hall, 1977).

Losoncy, Lewis E. & Donald W. Scoleri, *The New Psy-Cosmetologist: Blending the Science of Psychology Cosmetology* (Reading, PA: People-Media, 1985).

Lordahl, Jo Ann, *100 Affirmations for Creative People* (Bradenton, FL: Target Publishing, 1998).

Levinson, Jay Conrad, Rick Frishman, Michael Larsen & David L. Hancock, *Gorilla Marketing for Writers* (New York: Morgan James Publishing, 2001, 2010).

McGraw Phil C, *Real Life: Preparing for the 7 Most Challenging Days of Your Life* (New York: Free Press, 2008).

Morgenstern, Julie, *Time Management from the Inside Out* (New York: Henry Holt, 2000).

Osmond, Marie, *With Marcia Wilke, Might as Well Laugh about It* (New York: Penguin Group Double Day, 2009).

Pauley, Jane, *Skywriting: A Life out of the Blue* (New York: Random House, 2004).

Richie, George, *Return from Tomorrow.* (Grand Rapids: Baker Book House, 1978).

Ross, Marilyn & Tom Ross, *Jump Start Your Book Sales* (Buena Vista, CO: Communications Creativity, 1999).

Scheinfeld, Amram, *Why You Are You* (New York: Associated Press, 1970).

Sichel, Mark, *Healing from Family Rifts* (New York: McGraw-Hill, 2004).

Wells Joel, *Coping in the 80's* (Chicago, IL: The Thomas Moore Press, 1986).

ABOUT
the AUTHOR

S herri Mills has been a hairdresser for over forty-five years. She has had her own salon long enough to see life happen before her very eyes. She has listened to real-life problems and followed real-life outcomes—successes and failures—and through several generations, longer and more extensively than marriage counselors can.

In her practice she has seen the pain from too many divorces that didn't have to happen. She has been obsessed with trying to save as many marriages as she can.

Sherri's first book, *I Almost Divorced my Husband, but I Went on Strike Instead*, was written to women, with detailed instructions on how to deal with the double duty and double standard of householder work and instructions on how have more appreciation for their own husbands.

Men wanted instructions of their own so Sherri outlined in this book real solutions to issues that sabotage marital accord. The book is written in such a manner as to make sense to the male partner in the marriage.